WELL ENOUGH

Finding Health Despite the Wellness Industry

DEREK BERES

Print: 979-8-9954307-0-4
Digital: 979-8-9954307-1-1

Some names have been changed for privacy.

ALSO BY THE AUTHOR

Conspirituality: How New Age Conspiracy Theories Became a Health Threat (with Matthew Remski and Julian Walker)

Hero's Dose: The Case for Psychedelics in Ritual and Therapy

Global Beat Fusion: The History of the Future of Music

To Courtney, who is stronger than I can ever imagine

"To write is to carve a new path through the terrain of the imagination, or to point out new features on a familiar route."

Rebecca Solnit, *Wanderlust: A History of Walking*

CONTENTS

THE BODY IN CRISIS

1

I awake to find her staring into my eyes.

Her face, a mixture of relief, concern, confusion. An intimate moment between strangers, even if I don't recall how I ended up in her lap. My view broadens. Hers aren't the only eyes fixated on me. I've somehow grabbed the attention of the entire room. And I'm lying flat on the ground.

Let's backtrack. I hop into Jill's car after teaching yoga on the Upper East Side. She navigates to the east village. A ritual, by now. She takes my Tuesday evening class, drives us back to Jersey City. Sometimes we're hungry. We'll swing by Angelica Kitchen for cornbread and barley tea or that pizza joint on 2nd Ave. Tonight we met her friend at Caravan of Dreams, a popular basement restaurant on 6th St.

Seated in the backroom. A few glasses of wine find their way to our table. I take a sip. Suddenly the gravity of the universe rushes into my head. My heart palpitates; my skin feels clammy. Background music rushes to the forefront of consciousness. Table conversation now a foreign tongue, as if they're speaking through a cylinder hundreds of feet away.

The edges of sight become blurry. A feeling I know all too well: the onset of a panic attack.

I still don't know how to deal with them. Avoidance techniques don't work in public, not when they emerge this quickly, with this much aggression. An overwhelming feeling of impending death steals my attention, hijacks my physiology. Over a decade of this shit by now. Two have sent me to an emergency room, in New Brunswick, in Hackensack. I know them by their signatures yet am clueless as to why or how they emerge. Sometimes months pass without a sign. Sometimes, they attack more frequently. This one, more intense than most. I'm usually given a heads-up. A tingle, that weird intrusion on my forehead, an immediate, terrifying theft of breath. It always comes down to respiration. An arresting inability to pull air into my lungs. This one's not fucking around.

You probably know it as fight or flight. A more appropriate term is fight-flight-freeze. When alone, freezing is common. I'll curl into a ball on my bed, on the floor, thinking I can breathe my way through it. In public, I usually run for shelter. In this case, the tiny bathroom in the middle of the restaurant. I don't say a word to my old friend or the new one. Instead, I stand up, walk about eight feet to the lane between tables, turn left to bolt toward the bathroom door. The world spins faster, and faster. I'm rapidly being sucked down a drain, a single point of light receding. My mind slipping, desperately scrambling for some kind of grip, but there's no traction to be found. Just free fall. Then, nothing. Until I see her eyes.

I'll never learn her name. I'll only remember how embarrassed I feel, returning to consciousness in this poor woman's lap. Stranger still: she's 15 feet from my point of departure. I almost made the bathroom but have no idea how. I blacked out across the room.

The story is pieced together. Once seated again, Jill says I stood up quickly, silently, scurrying away. Accustomed to my odd behaviors, only murmurs and gasps alerted her to my actual condition. A woman approaches our table. We met the previous week through a mutual friend; she recognized me when I stood up. A neuroscientist, she knew something was wrong. So she tracked my movements. Somehow my subconscious will propelled me forward even though everything had gone black. Turns out I didn't reach the bathroom doorway. I walked straight into the wall, bounced off it, collapsing first onto a table, then onto the woman's lap. Stunned, she eased me onto the ground, following my limp body so I wouldn't hit my head. And some claim New Yorkers aren't courteous.

The neuroscientist gives me her number in case I want to talk through this. I thank her, still embarrassed, grateful those missing steps are stitched together. Not that I know what the fuck to make of it. I've long masked fear behind stoicism while remaining silent about my problems with anxiety. I didn't tell a soul, back then, save my sister, who also deals with them. Our forebears, too, and her kids. One stressed lineage.

I'm frustrated as hell. I move people for a living but can't figure out what moves me. I'd rather pass out in public than talk about it. Instead, I black out or flee parties without the courtesy of a goodbye, leaving friends wondering what the fuck is going on.

That changes with time. Eventually, I opened up about anxiety disorder, even other confidential conditions, like the eating disorder I struggled with for 15 years—and the link between the two. The project is a years-long process. Still ongoing.

That night in Caravan of Dreams, the only time I've blacked out in 50 years, opened my eyes to how little I understood my body. I vowed to learn as much about it as possible, devouring books, articles, and studies, spanning biology, physiology, anatomy, anthropology. To know more about my body, I had to understand how bodies become bodies to begin with. I put aside music journalism to pursue health and science writing. Eventually, health podcasting, with an emphasis on the rampant misinformation plaguing our time.

I slowly discovered a framework to discuss my body openly with others, my fears, concerns, triumphs and failures. I learn my quirks are shared with others, like misophonia, an oddly crippling condition in which the sound of others chewing makes me want to rush out of the room or punch something hard, or both. I consider how this plays into anxiety disorder as well, offering me different points of entry for understanding.

As I open up and express my body, people reply with the reality of their own. I realize my body isn't the only factor in my state of being. Health is a shared endeavor. Trapped inside a prison of physiology though I may be, it dawns on me that all health is public. Mine is as dependent on everyone else's as everyone else's is on mine. The cage door was open this entire time. I just finally learned how to step through.

I should have known better, given how engrained in consciousness this idea already was. While studying Buddhism in college, I was enamored with the concept of interdependence. Indra's net, everything connected, individuals like tiny jewels shining a light on all other jewels. The concept became a philosophical pursuit. Upon exploring the sciences, I began seeing interdependence as a biological and social truth as well. A common sentiment in the wellness industry I end up working in, *we're all one people*, took on a new dimension. Plenty of problems emerge from this view, like thinking all things are equal for everyone. I'll get into that.

Through talking to hundreds of experts as a writer and podcaster, I began viewing health not as an individual pursuit, but a public endeavor. Everything affects health: the environment, relationships, careers, all of it. The spark of revelation was my own body, a slow unfurling. Knowing others deal with their shit the way I deal with my own, I became comfortable divulging the strange intimacies of orthorexia, a selective eating disorder guided by a psychological fear of impurities. I started talking publicly about my struggles with anxiety, now aware so many others battle it themselves. I learned about the many entanglements and codependencies between personal and public health, how you can't have one without the other.

Strangely, the wellness industry I devoted so much of my life to doesn't see it that way. Their myopic focus on individual health, represented by the ascension of Robert F Kennedy, Jr's Make America Healthy Again (MAHA) movement to social and political power, became one of the worst things for health imaginable.

Before we get to the politics of wellness, we have to go back to the injury that started the clock. The restaurant blackout taught me about the sudden, terrifying loss of psychological control. The cage door was indeed open, but physiology still had me trapped.

The exact moment I learned the body is a fragile, unpredictable thing.

2

I'm wide open.

Charlie tosses me the ball. A perfect throw, fitting from a star Little League pitcher turned quarterback for our schoolyard football game. I catch it, turn to run. A few feet along, I completely lose traction. My legs give out as my sneakers slip on a patch of wet leaves. The Joyce Kilmer playground had not yet recovered from last night's November rain. A total, terrifying loss of physical control. At just that moment, Mike grabs my right shoulder to pull me down.

I don't hear the snap. I certainly feel it.

"Shake it off" rings in my head, advice every coach offers.

I give it a shot, pretending what just happened didn't really happen. My left leg momentarily agrees with gravity. Halfway into this expedition, my right leg collapses. It hits me though I have no idea what it is. That's what shock does to you.

I'm not sure how long I'm on the ground. I'm later told it took 20 minutes for the rescue squad to arrive. I vividly recall the technicians pulling jacket upon jacket from my immobile body, even though I can't remember my sixth-grade class-mates piling them on top of me. They gently place me on the stretcher. Off I go.

Enlightenment descends in Robert Wood Johnson's emer-gency room. The doctor has to straighten out my leg. Sound and fury attack, like a playing card jammed into a bike wheel. I scream as he yanks. Aromas of Clorox and formaldehyde drift through awareness. Probably sweat, maybe my own, maybe theirs. I've been conscious this entire time though my body is not my own. A feeling I'll experience often in the coming months.

Then I see it, the same drill we use to bore birdhouse holes in shop class. Only this one is going to ram a metal rod through my right leg, just above the knee, in order to hold my leg in traction. I'll be conscious during this procedure as well. A nurse stacks towels over my chest to shield me from watching the operation. Six pricks assault my leg, which quickly feels foreign. Not numb enough to avoid knowing a rod is being drilled through uninterrupted flesh and muscle.

This is what it takes to force biology to knit back together. Traction. A brutal, mechanical grounding in reality. A feeling I'll spend the rest of my life seeking out, through the gears of a bicycle, the deep roots of a yoga pose, the hard data of a clinical trial. While the wellness grifters I'd later encounter constantly tried to sell the illusion of floating above it all, I learned at 11 years old that survival requires traction.

Also vivid is the blood-soaked gurney left behind as they lift me onto the bed that will be home for the next month.

And the second-floor room in the pediatrics ward I'm wheeled into. Also, urinating all over myself. I've never been so drugged in my life, the boundary between autonomic and voluntary dissolved.

This is how they treat a broken femur in 1986. Well, part of the method: for eight weeks after traction I'll lie immobile in a full body cast. For this, I'm sent home. My nanny spends weekdays taking care of me, resulting in me becoming extremely knowledgeable about soap operas. Today, if you break your femur, doctors strap a breathable cast over your leg and have you walking the next day. Orthopedic surgeons eventually realized blood flow is more relevant to healing than immobility. I suffered the consequences of their ignorance for years. An important point that informed my understanding of medicine: knowledge evolves. We're not always the beneficiary in hindsight.

Suffering wasn't limited to recovery. Living in a hospital is traumatic. At one point, the skin around my right pin hole becomes infected. A nurse cuts away the skin surrounding the rod with a pair of blunt scissors to release the pus. The scar on that side remains noticeably larger to this day.

Then there's the matter of the bowel. You have to move in order for there to be movement. I was regularly fed laxatives to compensate for my lack of mobility. Graduated to enemas upon returning home. Those soon stopped working. And so every few days my father inserted an enema into my asshole, waited for it to drain into the bedpan, put on a latex glove, then manipulated his fingers to manually pull the shit from my colon. No matter how closely he cuts his fingernails, blood is inevitable.

My father and I had our issues. Some physical abuse in the years leading up to this accident, mostly involving a belt whipped across my ass. After graduating from college, walking in downtown Manhattan, I asked why he did that. He tells me he didn't know how to relate to children. Same type of shit his dad did to him, a cycle stuck on repeat on both sides of my family. Our ancestors fled impending world wars from Russia, Hungary, Poland. Quiet, stoic, bitter men who managed large families in part by releasing their inner rage on those closest to them. Quite a different understanding of "care" at that time. You cared for your family by providing survival necessities: shelter, clothing, food. Emotional well-being wasn't really a thing.

Cycles repeat if you don't address them. The breaking of my femur shifted my relationship with my father. We were both forced to reassess our notions of care. He certainly lived up to the moment. We remain close friends.

While the memory of my father ensuring I never suffer rectal prolapse or fecal impactions remains strong, another is stuck in my cranium. The strangest consequence of this entire debacle involves my unconscious self.

Night terror is a type of parasomnia—sleep disorders that provoke abnormal behaviors, movements, perceptions, or dreams. The "terror" is linked to an intense fear exhibited by rapid heartbeats, sweating, and screaming. The first occurs a few hours after arriving at the hospital. My sister slept curled in a chair next to me that evening. She said I woke up and pulled myself nearly upright using a swinging bar placed above my chest, there to help me lift parts of my body so nurses could change the bedsheets. Never in that entire month did I achieve anything resembling verticalness, yet Dawn swears I was close to touching my chest to my leg, which freaked her out. Not nearly as much as what I said to her, eyes wide open: "You look like you're from Bakersfield." I have no clue how I even knew about that city. Decades later, passing through the Central Valley while speeding from Los Angeles to San Francisco, I'm reminded of this night.

In traction, immobile, asleep letting wild machinations fly. Yet I'd never recall a thing the next morning, the screaming, the kicking, calling people on the phone. No clue how I pulled that one off. Except once, when I woke up chatting with my mother. *I'm awake*, I assure her. *You've said that before,* she rebuts. *No, this time I'm really awake. You've said that, too.* I remember the conversation the next morning, along with a feeling of paralysis in my unbroken leg.

What's worse, my outbursts were on public display. The nurses kept a log. I would scream eight, nine, a dozen times a night. I felt horrible for the children I kept awake, screaming into the void. They were dealing with their own shit. Here I am, not knowing how to deal with mine, even if it wasn't "me."

The terror calms when returning home. Occasional screams, not every night. They finally stop when the cast is removed and I return to the race of bipeds. Sort of. Three months in bed does a number to a body. Another six pass before I regain the ability to walk without the assistance of a crutch. I spent the entirety of sixth grade in home schooling. The overwhelming amount of time is devoted to wondering how such tragedy could befall anyone.

The experience also kicked off my insatiable desire to know as much as possible about the human body. Not just how it works, but how it breaks.

Nine years later, I'd get a front-row seat to that breaking point as a college student picking up shifts in the very same hospital.

3

I don't know how anyone develops a $40,000-a-month cocaine habit. Bob found a way.

He had it all: a wife he loved, kids he adored, a successful small business in East Brunswick, friends to go out drinking with after a hard week's work. So yeah, Bob still drank with his buddies, hanging onto the college days. Not all the time, of course. Then one of his friends brought cocaine into the mix. The cravings hit hard, man. The coke ruined everything. His wife, kids, business, gone. Deep in debt. He had it all until he didn't, which was the night he slit his wrist and tried to bleed out. Only he slit it wrong, which I hear is somewhat common.

Bob doesn't strike me as someone who wants to kill himself. He's too animated, too reflective, too lively. Too talkative, but that's fine. Underneath all these qualities is pain he can't reconcile, can't wrap his head around. Like a thought on the tip of your brain that won't come out. It's right there but somehow you can't see it.

I'm not trying to see it for Bob. Not my job. The job I have is to make sure he doesn't flee or complete what brought him into the hospital in the first place. What Bob craves is for someone to listen to him, even a 19-year-old Rutgers student he never met before. I'll do, at least for this shift. Then my replacement will likely do as well.

I don't know what his life is really like. All I have is his perspective, his lens, passions, failures, sense of right and wrong, biases, hidden and discovered. And stories. Bob has tons of them. Most patients are too drugged up or shot out to say much at all. Some ramble incoherently. Some yell, some cry, most sleep. Bob just talks, eight hours straight. That's fine, it's part of being a patient monitor. We were never instructed on whether or not to give advice, though I certainly don't. I'd been in pain before. But never *that* kind of pain. I'm not going to pretend to know how to navigate such a dark space.

Neither does Bob, it seems. How else do you end up in the emergency room after attempting to end it all? Who called the paramedics? Was he found writhing in his own blood somewhere? Did he want to be found, or just fade away like all his bad memories? I never know the mechanics of what lands someone here. I never ask. I only know they're here, and I'm here to make sure they stay put.

Sometimes I'm in the room with them. Sometimes, my chair's positioned within view in the hallway. Usually when they're violent, unpredictable. A few are strapped to the gurney. I'm right next to Bob. He's no threat, to others, at least. He's also detoxing from months of cocaine abuse, so maybe I caught him at the right moment, before his physiology betrays him.

The perks: I'm paid to study. Six dollars an hour, three shifts a week, reading textbooks and writing papers while strangers bleed out next door. The bad: hearing doctors and nurses banter about patients. Don't get me wrong, most healthcare professionals are kind. The ER is just hell to work in. You're stuck under fluorescent lights, chaos always erupting or threatening to, the smell of death everywhere. You leave reeking of bleach and misery.

Once in a while I catch the dark side. A nurse sneaks into a locked pharmacy closet because they're working a 30-hour shift and no human can pull off such a feat without assistance. A doctor laughing about patients with colleagues right after feigning compassion inside the room. Blood splattered on the floor after a gunshot victim is wheeled by at blinding speed. Being inside the room brings you closer to someone who, despite the luck of timing or incompetence, no longer wishes to inhabit the world you share. The ER holds the worst pains humans can possibly feel. Employees are expected to let it slide off their skin.

After two years working long shifts, I'm jaded, cynical, confused. Incapable of empathy. I don't know how feeling for others is even possible and I'm just an observer. To be around that much pain on the daily and not close yourself off seems impossible. You have to put up a wall or risk carrying that pain with you. Some are built for this type of work, sure. I've seen it: as a patient, when I lived there; as a patient monitor on the other side. Champion levels of compassion. They figured out how to contain the sadness, somehow.

Bob is an easy one, relatively speaking. There's Device, who lives on the streets of New Brunswick. I'm not sure how many times he ends up in the hospital. I am sure it's not a small number. One day he speaks at me for over an hour about how he created the universe. Considering I'm studying religion for my degree, I'm amazed at the coherence of his mythology. Something's off, though. Device believes he's the godhead directing all of it, everything, from big bang to this day. Strip that away and his tale is as rich and symbolic as any text considered sacred. After an hour or so, he stands on his bed, rips off his hospital gown, pisses all over the sheets. I spend the rest of my shift outside the room.

There was the heroin addict who taunted me relentlessly about my doctor father and the wealth that awaits me. (My father isn't a doctor; no wealth awaits me.) She's eventually strapped down because she desires nothing more than to sink her claws into my face. An elderly woman who swears to god that I'm the son she hasn't spoken to in decades. I assure her that's not the case. Doesn't matter. She spirals, cries turning into wails. Nurses sedate her. My boss puts me on another patient. I have a hard time falling asleep that night.

I'm given other duties on days when no patients await me. Wheeling patients to and from the catheter lab is common, as is running prescriptions. Sometimes I land the vaunted switchboard job, where you don't have to deal with emergencies. On occasion I wheel dead bodies to the morgue. Always fully wrapped by the time I arrive, they're just weight. If you think too hard about it, you realize it's the weight of a lifetime. So you try not to think too hard about it.

The morgue is cold, hell cold. Shoved in the basement, out of sight, a special card to access. Don't want randos waltzing in. Buckets of body parts soaked in formaldehyde stacked against the wall. Outside the building I'm studying the numerous forms of transcendence the world's religions inspire, endless takes on the body and soul, debates on the afterlife, the movement of poetry from learned voices to hungry, hopeful ears. Inside, I learn that life ends when consciousness ceases. With any luck the detritus of muscle and flesh and fat nourish the soil. Any construction of self these former bodies housed live on only in memory and hearsay.

Usually I work the seven-to-three shift. I'm an early riser.

My father never mentally left the navy. He considered seven "sleeping in" on the weekends. During the week, when school started at 8:30, I'm shaken awake at six to "get ready." I'm accustomed to rising with the sun in college. I stack all my classes early and pick up shifts on off days. I take the three-to-eleven shift sometimes, to force myself to study. Once in a while the hospital requests I cover the eleven-to-seven. My roommate, Wayne, loves it, little night owl he is. Not so for me. You're given a comfy reclining lounger and told the only thing you absolutely cannot do is fall asleep. Lights are dim, or off. Patients sleep. Impossible to focus on boring textbooks. Pay is the same, so what are we really doing here?

Not every overnight is chill, to be clear. Weekend shifts tend to explode. One moment I'm melted into the cushions trying to make sense of Buddhist texts, the next rushing a flailing kid into the trauma center. My age, drank himself into a violent altered state. Alcohol toxicity. A nurse rushes up, calls his name. I ask how she knows him. He's here every few weeks, she says. Nonchalant. Unattached. Just stating facts. There are many ways to kill yourself, many paths to desiring death. Not everyone transcends.

The night ends. I walk into the brisk morning air, cranky and discombobulated. Eight sleepless hours and a lifetime of uncertainty ahead, a life that I know can end without a moment's notice. I walk a few hundred feet to my Somerset St apartment, clamber up a flight of stairs, and pretend that I'll sleep, knowing that will never happen.

You don't spend two years under fluorescent lights watching strangers bleed out and casually brush off the scent of cleaning solution and unrealized dreams. The trauma follows you home. It settles into your bones and rewires your nervous system to always anticipate the next disaster.

4

Insomnia becomes a lifestyle when you realize how easily the machinery can break. A few years later, in Hackensack, I'm still not sleeping, though for an entirely different reason.

I gather all the contraband, shove it in a plastic bag. A few glass pipes, wood bowl, the plastic bong that still smells of cheap weed. Stuff the bag below the sink, sliding it through a gaping hole in the cheap particleboard. *What if they bring a dog?* pops into my head, so I rush downstairs, fling the shopping bag into the dumpster. Who knows what horrors my beloved accoutrements discover. The cleaners I live above dump toxic solutions into the same receptacle. One thing is certain: no police dog is gonna sniff that out.

None of this was necessary. A good hour passes between me thinking I'm having a heart attack and the ambulance showing up in the parking lot on Route 17. My first solo apartment is a Hackensack studio built on top of Classic Cleaners. $600 a month to live directly above machinery used to sanitize clothing, plus whatever chemicals seep through the poorly built infrastructure. Only four apartments in this complex, one occupied by a friend who's also a weed dealer, now my weed dealer. At this moment, a decision I regret.

The night started out fine. In preparation for meeting Darren in Hoboken, I take a few rips from the bong. Everything starts spiraling. A feeling I've had before, often, though this one rushes at me with unusual vigor. Tight chest, wandering brain. Heart palpitations galore. I'm going to die on the side of a highway at 22 years of age.

I know I'm calling the ambulance, and I know they'll know what's going on, a prophecy that kinda sorta turns out true. They won't learn the full story, both what I won't tell them and what none of us know. Dash around my studio frantically, gather things, throw shit out, clean, the latter an odd but recurring choice whenever I have a panic attack. Focusing on a task proves helpful when overtaken by an avalanche of anxiety. Scrubbing dishes and vacuuming have worked before. Not tonight.

Even the dispatcher sounds skeptical. I'm more frantic than dying. She sends an ambulance at my insistence. The studio still reeks of weed as I carry the cordless phone (look it up) to the parking lot. Of course a cop shows up first. There are protocols for this type of thing. He really wants to get inside my apartment, you know, to "check things out." I know what he's doing, he knows that I know, and he's forcing the issue anyway. I punt, he knows I'm punting, but I'm a white guy in Hackensack and he's not going to take liberties he might have with others. The phone comes with me to the emergency room.

The rescue squad attached oxygen to my nose. Immediate calm washes over me. Halfway to the hospital I just want to turn around. I'm embarrassed, they're pissed, rushing out on a Friday evening to shuffle this kid who's on who knows what to the ER when they could be enjoying a pizza and watching the game. The doctor is even less forgiving. He treats me with as little respect as possible. I can't blame him, though I also know it's not just weed. Bong hits triggered something but weren't the origin of that thing.

I won't piece this together for years when I'm officially diagnosed with general anxiety disorder. Only then do I finally understand what's been crashing my nervous system since my first panic attack sent me to Robert Wood Johnson (yeah, there again) at age 16.

They didn't know what was happening back then either. Panic attacks weren't in the public vernacular. I had gotten in a fight with my mom, sprinted around the block in a tizzy, returning home to collapse on the bathroom floor. She freaks out, rightly. Suddenly the entire neighborhood is watching me being rolled out on a stretcher. The doctors in New Brunswick treat me with kindness and respect because I'm a kid and there's a corroborating witness. Plus, no marijuana. The Hackensack doctor likely thinks it's worse than weed, as in opioid worse, though he never considers a panic attack. The year is 1998, after all, when most people didn't really diagnose them, especially when substances are involved.

Which is a shame. When I first learned about anxiety disorder, panic attacks were presented as being "all in your head." While a grain of truth exists—there are techniques some people (including myself) can do to help alleviate the existential distress of an attack—the origin of the physiological reaction remains a mystery. That doesn't make them any less real.

An important piece of this story helped drive my panic. I was heavy into the poetry and theater scene. One of my favorite professors at Rutgers was Miguel Algarin, who cofounded the Nuyorican Poets Cafe in Alphabet City. I performed all over North Jersey and New York City. I also did spoken word with a band. A useful distraction, as I had just gone through the first major breakup of my life. There's a photo of me from a show at Webster Hall, mic in hand, looking like a ghost. At six-three, I had dropped to 159 pounds. The breakup hit me hard and I wasn't taking care of myself. While I did put weight back on, this marked the beginning of a 15-year struggle with disordered eating.

Which, it turns out, helps explain how I ended up in the emergency room in Hackensack.

5

The logic is simple: everything you ingest must meet specific macronutrient percentages. If a block of tofu provides this percentage of protein, I need a comparable fat source, slightly more carbohydrates. The Zone Diet provided numbers to shoot for: 30% protein, 30% fat, 40% carbohydrates. Here I am, in my kitchen, manically reading labels, hopping on my dial-up internet connection (look it up) to find analytics on produce, trying to achieve that magic number.

The process often leads to such frustration that I don't eat at all. Better to forgo a meal than consume the "wrong" number of macros. Magically, the founder of Zone sells a whole lot of products with the "right" percentages. The perfect accompaniment to his books, which are packed with sciencey data. To accompany a months-long depression following my breakup, I chose this diet to nourish me. As you can imagine, it wasn't very nourishing.

Food is a deeply personal topic; nutrition advice is rampant. Not an ideal combination, especially when offered by people who have no idea what they're talking about. The person most likely to buy a self-help book has already bought several. Same holds for diet books, which should clue us in to the efficacy of either. This was the case in the nineties, so just imagine how social media exploded the number of self-proclaimed nutritionists (which is not a protected term in America), exploiting an incessant desire to eat as "clean" as possible.

The Zone kicked off a brutal, decades-spanning era of disordered eating, a condition that evolved over time as my selection of foods became more and more limited. Being in "the zone" eventually became a quest for eating the most wholesome, "pure" foods. I cycled through many identities around eating: pescatarian, vegetarian, keto. While living in Los Angeles, I maintained what I believe is a relatively healthy vegan diet for nearly two years. That led to regular gastrointestinal issues, though, so who knows.

Even at my supposedly healthiest, selective dieting is still involved. Body dysmorphia remains. I'm not getting enough calories to support my schedule, as I crash on occasion. Panic attacks linger. I never link anxiety to diet. I never suspect that what put me in the emergency room is related to my neuroses around food.

My initial struggles with eating occurred just as my yoga practice really picked up. I'm working eight-hour days in midtown Manhattan, then hustling downtown to the Movement Salon or Jivamukti Yoga for an evening class. My body was a bit of a mess by this point. Alongside the fractured femur, I broke my right collarbone when flipping over the handlebars of my bicycle and twice snapped my right ankle playing basketball. These insults resulted in serious bodily imbalances that hundreds of chiropractic sessions never really addressed (though did temporarily alleviate pain). For the first time since the body cast, yoga provides actual structural relief to chronic issues. Leaving my Hackensack studio at 7:30 am and returning home after 8 pm seems like a small price to pay for getting my body back, though leaving my insane orange tabby, Sakyamuni, alone for so long isn't great.

Depending on how you approach the practice, yoga is not necessarily only a set of postures. In tow is an entire collection of practices designed to cultivate a particular worldview. How much of this is "ancient" is debatable given modern yoga is a late 19th-century invention. A lot of romantic rewriting has been injected into the discourse. This was especially true in the nineties, well before social media tilted yoga in odd new directions, such as a pipeline for right-wing propaganda. One of the most discussed and debated aspects of the practice involves what you put into your body.

Much of the spiritual rhetoric I now criticize on my podcast, *Conspirituality*, is simply rehashed messaging from yoga lingo of the nineties, itself a modernized form of late sixties ideology. Not all of it is incorrect. What you put into your body matters. Eating fresh, whole foods is considered by dietitians to be a fantastic course of action (for those who can afford it). Needing to be vegetarian to practice yoga is questionable, though many follow that path to great success. Growing your own food is a nice idea, if available to you.

There's the ideal and the real, which often don't meet. Then there's simply the absurd. Some yoga instructors are really efficient at the latter. I was told that every food imaginable was toxic early in my practice. Nightshades like tomatoes, potatoes, and eggplants are to be avoided. Onions and garlic are *rajasic*, along with coffee, lemon, and eggs. Never consume them so you don't excite the senses. Oh wait, eggs are also *tamasic,* along with bread, vinegar, and reheated foods. They dull the senses. You don't need that. Oh wait, onions and garlic are in there, too. Depends on your constitution, which changes depending on who is unqualifiedly analyzing you. Depends on the time of day. Depends on whether or not you're on your moon cycle.

This is how I become orthorexic. Orthorexia isn't a clinical term; the closest parallel is avoidant/restrictive food intake disorder (ARFID). Still, I find the concept applicable to my experience. You become obsessed with purity, avoiding foods deemed impure or unhealthy. Who's deeming? Certainly not clinical nutritionists. This disorder is fueled by wellness coaches and yoga instructors who believe their anecdotes trump expert knowledge.

This isn't hyperbole. America has long endured anti-intellectualism, a trait that dovetails with the conceit of rugged individualism. These complementary qualities have trailed me throughout my decades in wellness spaces: the smug certainty that education is poison and power is compromise, so you have to educate and empower yourself. You *should* be doing both those things. Where you source information that educates and empowers matters. And this is where the conceit kicks in: despite all scientific evidence, contrarian wellness activists rage against prevailing wisdom. Nowhere is this trend more prevalent than when it comes to nutrition.

The same struggle that led me to obsessively count macros in Hackensack turned into a recurring battle in grocery store aisles throughout my decades of living in New York City and Los Angeles. Depending on what teacher I was studying with or, later, what health influencer was in my social media feed, I cycled through restrictions of this or that food or food group. While I believe veganism is a perfectly healthy diet for some people, my two-year stint happened in large part due to the idea that dairy is "toxic." One popular documentary claimed eggs are unhealthier than cigarettes. People believed it.

Early in my yoga days, meditating for world peace was common in New York City studios. Earnest instructors believed tuning a bunch of predominantly white folk into the planet's collective nervous system would alleviate the distress of suffering brown people half a world away.

This odd application of metaphysics really hit home one evening at Jivamukti, a studio credited with mainstreaming the Vinyasa style of yoga in America. The founders, Sharon Gannon and David Life, cut their teeth in the eighties-era punk scene, taking a contrarian approach to politics and holistic living that informed their longtime veganism. If you arrived at the studio wearing fur or leather, you were asked to leave. I appreciated that they stuck to their values even at the risk of losing revenue, watching more than one disgruntled New Yorker shuffle out in the dead of winter, muttering expletives not so under their breath.

Every New Year's Eve the studio hosted a silent meditation, serving up free chai to anyone who wanted to come sit in lotus, read a book, or lie on the ground. At midnight, Sharon led a call-and-response chant as the evening turned into a social event. One year, the chant was "I will be vegan," over and over and over, crooned while she stroked her harmonium. Never a big fan of kirtan, I sat eyes closed, enduring the audacity of this commitment while overstimulated from black tea. As a vegetarian, the notion of turning vegan didn't bother me. Her declaration that everyone on the planet must become one didn't sit right.

A few months later I visited Morocco for the first time. Beyond the health and fitness component of my life that is the focus of this book, I also worked as a global music journalist, DJ, and producer, twin careers that sometimes converged. In fact, alongside my partner in EarthRise Sound-System, Duke Mushroom, we remixed one of Sharon's songs. I also spun records for Jivamukti events and classes. As a longtime fan of Moroccan gnawa music, covering the country's sacred music festival was a dream come true. I visited four times over the next three years writing about music.

Strolling around the world's largest medina in Fez, I couldn't avoid the many meat shops displaying dismembered hoofs, heads, legs, and other chunks of carcass spread out on blankets on the ground. These shops are the heart of the local economy and provide the medina's one million residents with nourishment. That stupid chant kept reverberating in my head as I walked through the winding streets, quietly laughing at the absurdity of American yogis believing their dietary prescription is appropriate for everyone.

That didn't make the image of decapitated goats easy to view. The origins of my vegetarianism were ethical, with health a secondary consideration. (A bit of a shifting landscape that helped serve as cover for my eating disorder; sometimes health was the first consideration, or so I said.) What struck me most was the privilege occurring inside of a posh Manhattan yoga studio that blinded its adherents from recognizing the vantage points of others. Disparities were already embedded in the medina. One building impoverished, the adjacent structure owned by French speculators charging $500 a night to stay in an "authentic" riad. Local cafes serving steaming plates of couscous for under $5 sit next to upscale French-Moroccan restaurants charging $100 a plate. Colonization left a long legacy. Adding American demands under the guise of spirituality didn't make sense.

Pain is an integral component of veganism. The suffering of animals is a primary motivator for this lifestyle. Activist organizations weaponize images like those I witnessed in Fez to stir emotions and rally people to their cause. The effectiveness of such imagery is debated, though it certainly hits hard. But I can't shake the privilege of assumption, the idea that these million people living in the world's largest walled city need to abandon their practices to suit people an ocean away that are in a much better financial position to pursue such a lifestyle.

In 2003, cultural critic Susan Sontag published a book-length essay on the value and perils of pain imagery. The context was war photography, visuals of genocide splayed across television and print media. She reconsiders an earlier work that claimed such photography can "shrivel sympathy," arguing that images serve as a catalyst for deeper understanding and moral inquiry. Years before social media dominated the media landscape, Sontag was concerned with the "hyper-saturated" world of images leading to an "image-glut." This glut compels people to turn an eye from the context of the image, which becomes background noise. She observes that it's "absurd to identify the world with those zones in the well-off countries where people have the dubious privilege of being spectators, or of declining to be spectators, of other people's pain," concluding that "hundreds of millions of television watchers are far from inured to what they see on television. They do not have the luxury of patronizing reality."

And so two voices clashed in my head as I strolled through the medina. One, a distant whisper promising a better land when we abandon a feeding strategy other carnivorous animals never consider. The other, the many whose lives depend on consuming flesh and muscle advising me to knock myself down a few notches to where most of the world lives.

Wellness influencers tend to scream in the former voice at you. This goes beyond veganism. I hold no ill will toward the practice, and appreciate people who dedicate themselves to it, whether for health or ethics, or both. The demands adherents make is relevant to this story, however: the notion that *this* particular practice is toxic, so this *other* particular practice must be an antidote, drives much of the frenzy and paranoia baked into wellness thinking. Everything becomes a binary even as the end goal is not: drive people into an ideology.

A few years after Morocco, I went on my first date with my now-wife, Callan. At this point I'm fully vegan in Los

Angeles. Veganism isn't foreign to her. She tried it while living in New York. She even attended the same Jivamukti classes. Like me, she was also a yoga instructor. Her carnivorous diet didn't bother me. I never went the "everyone must be vegan" route. And she was willing to date a vegan…for a while.

Old habits die hard. Sometimes they rush back with undeniable force. Pizza finally cracks me. I always knew this delicacy would do me in. You don't grow up in Jersey and forsake a state treasure: thin crust, oil running onto the paper plate, just the right crunch and perfect elasticity of cheese. We'd eat vegan pizza at Sage in Culver City. Which isn't pizza. You can't pile a bunch of vegetables on top of a cornmeal crust and desecrate language like that.

Speaking of language, I've been criticized that I was never *really* vegan. It's a lifestyle, I'm told, a set of ethics, a way of existing. Definitely *not* a diet. If identifying a way of eating with a way of being is your thing, cool. Just don't expect to win people over with purity tests. You become an easy mark for ridicule. Even today, most of my diet is vegetarian. I regularly cook vegan dishes. Just because I'm not committed to a movement's principles doesn't mean I don't share some of them. As it turned out, not being vegan turned out a lot healthier for me, mentally and physically.

Here's how my perspective shifted: Bulletproof Coffee founder Dave Asprey and fitness blogger Mark Sisson discussed their longstanding battles with stomach problems during two separate podcast episodes. Chronic gas, bloating, diarrhea, and energy depletion issues were solved, they claim, with a ketogenic diet. Having experienced similar issues for years, these episodes landed like a revelation.

I told Callan that I was ready, after nearly 20 years of abstinence, to integrate meat back into my diet. A few days later, we ordered a whole branzino at a (now defunct) Mexican-Moroccan fusion restaurant called Briks in downtown LA. A few more nights pass. Friends order a Japanese steak for the table at a sushi restaurant. I dig in.

Growing up a latchkey kid in the eighties, most of my meals were microwaved. Salisbury steak and chicken TV dinners were regular fuel. There were these things called MicroMagic cheeseburgers. You remove the plastic wrap from the burger and stick the entire thing, bun, cheese, meat and all, wrapped in a paper towel into the microwave. The result was a soggy mess. MicroMagic fries were no better. Believe it or not, there was a milkshake. I'm certain my body was at least 10 percent MicroMagic by the end of the eighties.

My father ends up becoming a prolific cook and baker. Now in his eighties, he regularly texts me photos of his latest creation. My mom, not so much, though she was always an incredible baker. As two working parents, my diet came entirely from frozen cardboard boxes. By the time I stopped eating beef at 19, I'd never eaten a proper steak. Sinking my teeth into the Japanese version is sensory overload.

The break wasn't entirely clean. I returned to carnivorism with more restrictions. The keto diet closed my feeding window to six hours a day. Thankfully, this only lasted about two months. I quickly observed the same neurotic thinking around macros, only now it's about time. Waiting until noon to have my first bite of food was miserable. After a few weeks of "powering through," I'm still hangry, which isn't great for my morning yoga classes or my own workout. Keto, it turns out, provided the last dying embers of disordered eating. I abandoned any form of dieting in early 2015 and have never looked back.

But change happened. My stomach issues cleared up in a few weeks, as described in those podcasts. There's more. I've battled recurring outbreaks of canker sores since a teenager. After a few months of eating meat, they ceased coming with the same vigilance and speed. One arrives instead of six. Once I start taking lysine and vitamin B, they nearly disappear.

My fatigue is also gone. The biggest and most surprising

consequence of eating meat again, however, is the cessation of panic attacks. I can't explain the physiological reason. Sometimes, one will creep up, a distant crackling, a *hey, remember me*, like I used to get right before an attack. But the assault never arrives. For over a decade, I've been panic attack-free. My chronic anxiety hangs around. It just never becomes a chemical tornado.

I have no direct proof of causation. Correlation speaks for itself. In this case, it's enough for me. In nearly every regard, eating meat again is a healthier option, at least for me.

Emerging from this long stretch with disordered eating, I now see the signs everywhere. Consciously or not, the wellness industry, with all its purification and detoxification rituals, regularly promotes eating disorders like orthorexia. I don't believe it's a conscious decision. A lot of people caught up in it, even influencers promoting versions of it, aren't intentionally pushing people in that direction. But it is a consequence of their fixation with "clean" eating.

Demonizing ingredients and food groups, selectively removing more of them from your diet, risks developing an unhealthy relationship to food. It all stems from a desperate attempt to avoid suffering, a delusion that if you just micromanage your inputs perfectly, your body will never break or betray you.

Pain isn't something you can just optimize away. I learned that lesson early.

6

Why?

That question hangs over my bed for three months, persisting long after. A sort of religious fixation. During the acute phase of my broken femur, as my body tremors with pain that is barely, momentarily sedated with oxycodone, I writhe on my sweat-soaked bed asking whatever god my parents didn't instill in me why he would allow such a thing to happen. I was just a kid, after all. No one should experience such pain, or so I believed.

The extraordinary amount of pain overwhelms me. First, due to the broken leg. Then, from an immobile and atrophying body. I grew up playing every sport possible. Games are what my friends did. Bike rides were how I got everywhere in our Jersey suburb. I started walking to school in first grade, alone, the early eighties being peak latchkey generation. Between leaving for school shortly after dawn until the street lights came on, my parents rarely knew where I was or what I was doing. I certainly didn't tell them.

Hell is being unable to go about a normal day. With so many legitimate and suspect ways of addressing pain, I soon became aware that its alleviation is big business. As I aged, I grew curious as to what pain means, not only in my body but as a construct.

Raised agnostically Catholic (I told my parents I no longer wanted to attend CCD after I recovered; they shrugged and said "fine") my question to the invisible has a biological foundation. The Arabic word *'alam* describes a range of pain, from the longing for a beloved to the absolute misery of physical insults. In Islam, pain is considered part of God's will. A predestined part, even, guiding humans through the treachery of existence. While the Arabic world has long produced analgesics, true relief is achieved through prayer, contemplating the divine, reading sacred texts. In this context, pain is necessary for the spiritual path.

The question of *why* led me, eventually, to science. To wonder not just why pain happens, but how we're wired to process it. Early Arabic poetry, made famous to Americans through the transcendent writing of Rumi, often used pain to describe an intense yearning for communion with the divine. Eventually the West caught on, relating physical and emotional pain through evidence-based research. Acetaminophen, one of the most studied and effective interventions for physical pain, was found useful for alleviating social distress. This dynamic has been explored in Arabic and Asian literature for millennia. No surprise that alleviating one form of pain helps with others.

There's more. Pain is not only individual, but cultural. Depending on the culture you're born into, what is painful to someone else might not register as pain to you, and vice-versa. Incredibly, this includes physical pain. While research in this field is still developing, mirror neurons play an essential role in pain management. These specialized nerve cells activate when we perform an action; they also activate when we observe someone else performing an action. They've been implicated in empathy for pain, the perception of others' pain, even pain management in clinical scenarios.

Mirror neurons fire when you're in pain as well as when you watch someone else in pain. Enter the cultural piece: pain is a conditioned response. If your culture doesn't treat something as painful, your mirror neurons won't register that action as painful. This sounds counterintuitive, though further research has investigated the role of emotions in pain. Pain centers in the brain triggered by physical insults are separate from an individual's affective response—how the emotion related to that pain is displayed. How you deal with physical pain depends on your emotional response as much as the insult itself.

Consider a subculture prominent in the American zeitgeist. The manosphere loves calluses, on their palms, over their hearts. Thin skin implies a weak constitution. Tears streaming down cheeks, a betrayal. Tears in muscle, glory. Pain is to be overcome, not a signal something's amiss. The only acceptable emotion is a relentless drive forward and all the collateral damage that entails.

This mind over matter, pain at all costs mentality is experiencing a renaissance in modern America. Never went away, but therapy is an increasingly common option among men. Thanks, Tony Soprano and Kendrick Lamar. In the bro fitness space, though, manning up still means invoking your inner bear to plow through life's challenges. This contrasts sharply with the experience of many women, who are more open to the benefits of therapy to manage pain, and whose pain has historically been undervalued by a medical industry dominated by, until recently, men.

As with anything, there's a wide range of responses when it comes to dealing with pain. Chronic pain sufferers are often unaware of the etiology of their insults, which frustrates the entire process and can lead to more pain. Ignorance is certainly not bliss in such cases. As we've covered on *Conspirituality*, these sufferers can be more susceptible to the influence of wellness coaches who confidently declare they know what's wrong and how to treat it, even as they've earned no such knowledge. When you're desperate for solutions, the parasocial desire for confidence becomes its own drug.

Then there are people who literally don't feel pain, which is dangerous because they often don't seek help when their body is in distress. For those not in the extremes, pain is as social as it is physical. People with strong networks tend to feel less social distress than those without support, and so feel less pain overall.

There's another side to this: people who experience a lot of pain tend to empathize with the pain of others. During that year-long process of traction, body cast, and recovery, I received over 70 shots. (Your mind finds all sorts of things to occupy itself with when immobile; one of mine was counting.) Needles don't bother me when I'm getting a shot. But I can't watch a needle puncture someone else's skin, in real life or on a screen. I avert my gaze during every episode of *The Pitt*. My mirror neurons erupt like fireworks.

Experiencing pain doesn't make you empath of the year, however. Another double-edge: being in too much pain can close you off to the pain of others. Pain is complicated. Sometimes being in pain helps you recognize pain others experience. Sometimes, pain becomes a competition. *Oh, you think you're hurting? Live in my body a day.*

Managing expectations of pain, like feeling it, is both individual and social. Pain has boundaries, however, which the wellness world sometimes overlooks. Because of America's hyperindividualism, anecdotes become a guiding light for every ailment. The assumption: what heals me must heal you. Untrue, though compelling for those in pain, and to those who want to sell products to cure it. Pain reduced to a marketing vehicle.

Sometimes, the attempt to cure pain creates a new kind of performance. Which brings me to the most performative space of all.

THE PURITY HUSTLE

7

I don't know what the fuck is happening.

The lithe instructor barks minimal commands, sometimes in English, sometimes a foreign tongue. Everyone else comprehends the code switching, gracefully gliding through a series of rigorous postures with little effort. I'm constantly pausing to identify my right leg from my left. The humidity is stifling, which is apparently a feature. Avrami's latest thing is Jivamukti Yoga. Having studied yogic texts for years, I'm finally trying out the form. Completely lost, exhausted, overheating, enthralled.

Months pass before I begin practicing in earnest. New to New York, I'm earning $23,000 a year as a crossword puzzle editor. Whatever excess cash I can spare goes to capoeira lessons. Having dabbled in Tae Kwon Do in college, I'm intrigued by the martial art disguised as a dance. For about six months, I've been taking classes on the corner of 6th and 20th. The mestre speaks no English. I pick up whatever Portuguese necessary to make it through class, though memorizing the songs is taking longer.

Then I started beginner yoga at Movement Salon on 17th

and 3rd. Unlike the brightly-lit, mirror-filled studio at Jivamukti, this room feels like a dungeon. A welcoming one.
Carrie keeps the lights off, candles flickering, soft music, an
empathic voice. The perfect vibe, given where I am in my
movement education.

I don't recall every struggle of learning this anatomical
language. Just the repetition. Years of injuries unspooling.
Overlooked muscles manipulated in novel ways. Crying
every time I crawl into pigeon pose. Not bawling, more like
tears trickling out as the right leg I've broken three times is
finally being stretched. This pose hooks me. I'm healing.

Healing physically, emotionally, psychologically. They go
together, here and often. For the first time in forever I'm not
in constant pain. For years, I was subjected to weekly chiropractic sessions, starting at 16 due to sciatica. The femur break
left a long trail of bodily imbalances. Now I'm realizing that
fate is not sealed. I just haven't been using my body right.

A choice had to be made. I couldn't afford to split my
devotion. Capoeira or yoga. Both have vocabularies, spoken
and physical. With capoeira, I need to learn the songs, the
culture, the movement. Yoga is its own language. As much as
I love the martial art, my body yearns for yoga. The decision
is made.

Three weekly yoga classes trigger absolute devotion. Over
the next five years I'm in multiple weekly classes, workshops,
small groups in living rooms. I travel around the boroughs
sampling hatha, vinyasa, Bikram, kundalini, Anusara, whatever's on offer. By 2003, I'm in teacher training, ready to share
a practice I love deeply with the world. Or, at least the Movement Salon, the first studio to hire me after becoming
certified.

8

The poster is in every studio. A tiny figure makes his way
through a mind-boggling 908 postures, each with perfect

form. This devoted yogi created the Master Yoga Chart for his guru, Swami Kailashananda. Setting up a camera, sticking a remote under his tongue, assuming the position, triggering the camera, 908 times. An understatement. Who knows how many photos he reshot. That's just the start of it. Next, he cuts his lithe body from the photo and pastes each posture onto a large sheet of paper. That sheet has sold over 50,000 copies since 1984.

I see the dude everywhere, then discover his studio is just three blocks from the Movement Salon. Dharma Yoga Center was located on 3rd Ave for years, until Dharma Mittra moved to a larger space in Flatiron where, at age 86, he continues teaching multiple classes per week.

I'm a couple of years into my practice when first walking up the stairs. The sequence is unlike anything I've experienced. First pose: handstand. A Vinyasa flow, followed by a forearm stand. Flow. Another handstand, kicking up with the other leg. Flow, another forearm stand, flow, warrior poses. Intense. Yet non-competitive. Senior students move around the room helping novices. Most classes follow a rigorous, serious structure. This is spiritual Romper Room.

Then there's Dharma. I've never sought a guru, preferring to learn a little from a lot of people. Yet I understand why people dedicate themselves to his practice. I never hang around long enough to know the internal politics of his studio —and every studio has politics. One run-in with his handler proves he's fiercely protected, even if in the room he's open, kind, compassionate. One of the strongest yogis alive, yet never flaunts it. Sure, there's a famous *Vanity Fair* photo of Dharma rocking an armless headstand on top of a manhole cover in the meatpacking district. The position looks impossible, though he easily repeats it on the studio carpet from time to time.

Dharma's self-knowledge is matched by his awareness of his student's bodies. I've never been the most flexible yogi. Way more flexible than when I started, though today I focus more on mobility than flexibility. Yoga has always been a struggle. Forward bends are a pleasure; backbends are my bane. I can rock arm balances with ease, but after decades my glutes never reached the ground in pigeon. The idea of lotus makes my knees scream.

Physical adjustments have waned in American yoga culture. With numerous male instructors abusing female students, fewer teachers are willing to touch students. This was not the case at the turn of the 21st century. For better and worse, teachers regularly offered adjustments. I grew up in that culture, love the hands-on nature of yoga, and regularly adjusted students myself. I tried to be aware of limitations as I was adjusted too firmly on occasion. I walked into an Ashtanga studio in Miami, which was not my normal practice. The instructor was convinced that your palm should rest flat on the floor in side angle pose. She forced my hand into that position, tweaking my lower back. Another instructor at Jivamukti once pulled me up into bow pose with such force that I couldn't walk without pain for a week. This happens when instructors aren't paying attention to the student in front of them, thinking everyone should be pushed into postures as on the Master Yoga Chart.

Dharma's nothing like that. Having been adjusted by him numerous times, I'm amazed how he's forceful when appropriate and backs off when necessary. Sometimes, he manipulates my legs further into a split than I ever thought possible. Other times, he places a soft fingertip on my knee, gently suggesting the direction my leg should go.

While a fan, inherent skepticism never let me become an acolyte. During meditation workshops, we perform a bee buzzing sound for extended periods, which Dharma swears tunes us into the frequencies of the universe. We furiously rub our hands together before rubbing them over our closed eyes. The white spots are actual stars in the galaxy, he declares. When Dharma turned vegan, he strongly suggested everyone needs to do the same in order to practice authentic yoga, the same vibe that turned me away from Jivamukti.

I'm allergic to the very notion of "authentic yoga." Not that I didn't buy into the idea early on. If anything, searching for it is the closest I came to cult thinking. The moral righteousness got to me: the presumption that moving my body in a particular way and thinking particular thoughts was making the world a better place. Don't misunderstand: focusing on progressive ideas designed to help others is a great practice. It's just the presumption part: there's a way to do yoga *right*, and if you're not doing it that way, you're part of the problem.

I've gotten so much out of yoga, physically, emotionally, socially, over decades of practice. To this day, bickering about authenticity flags people way too invested in their own points of view. Inflexibility is not an ideal outcome of any practice.

If you haven't spent time in yoga spaces, this might sound weird. If you have, you know how quickly the vibe turns authoritarian. Some people enjoy feeling righteous more than being factual. Treating the body as a moral object has a long history of horrible outcomes, a phenomenon that took me years to work out.

In 2025, I was asked to write the Essay of the Week for *The Guardian* about how MAHA promotes body fascism. An editor heard an episode of *Conspirituality* where I discuss RFK Jr's soft eugenics. I received some pushback over the term, though it's not mine: "soft" eugenics is used in academia to distinguish blatant pogroms from the more manipulative kind of body fascism, such as telling people they have a chronic disease because they don't have the willpower to get healthy. Kennedy's movement falls into the latter camp. They're not calling for the execution of certain races. But the policies Kennedy has implemented and the rhetoric he espouses treat the death of unhealthy people like a shrug. Victim-blaming is rampant in MAHA circles.

We covered this topic in depth in our 2023 book, *Conspiri-*

tuality: How New Age Conspiracy Theories Became a Health Threat. In it, we gaze back at efforts in the late 19th century that promoted a similar mindset. While the romanticized version frames yoga as an ancient, peaceful practice, modern yoga is descended from anti-colonial struggle in which a powerful civic body is reflected in a strong individual body. Traditional yoga postures were combined with European weightlifting and gymnastics to form the basis of what is now practiced in studios worldwide.

This isn't a criticism of how yoga evolved. If you're struggling for independence against foreign rule, strengthening your body (and in the process, your mind and resolve) is a healthy response. Strength training in any situation is good, politics aside. In this case, it doesn't really matter if your favorite yoga class is rooted in a social struggle. But there are situations in which overt moralizing quickly turns toxic.

Consider a leading indicator of chronic disease: obesity. Wellness influencers have raged against fat forever. MAHA reinvigorated longstanding stigma against any sign of flab. As with the gamut of reactionary right-wing politics, the Kennedy's coalition often expresses a visceral hatred for the obese. Kennedy is only a symptom of a much larger problem in the wellness industry: the idea that if you're not in a position to eat "clean" and workout daily, fix your life; if you can't fix your life, don't come crying when you're in the hospital. And definitely don't expect us to pay for your coverage.

Health is never individual. And it's always political. Being overweight might have something to do with personal factors, or it might not. Public health experts place roughly half of health outcomes on individual actions, like diet and exercise. These practices matter. Other factors are equally important, however.

When it comes to obesity, factors to consider include: genetic predisposition; medical conditions, like hypothyroidism, polycystic ovary syndrome, Cushing's syndrome, and hypothalamic obesity; medications, including steroids, antidepressants, antipsychotics, diabetes medications, beta blockers, seizure medications, and birth control pills; aging, as muscle mass decreases naturally over time; poor sleep; chronic stress; economic status; built environment; work and time pressures.

For anyone facing these factors, "put down the soda and hit the gym" is a farce. Worse, it breeds shame when diet and exercise fail to move the scale, compounding their stress. Their health worsens under the weight of the blame.

Tragically, given his rise to political power, numerous bureaucrats now repeat Kennedy's language: fat chronic disease patients are increasing *your* premiums because you have to subsidize *their* shitty lifestyles. Never mind this is how insurance has always worked, with healthier citizens paying into a pool they may need to draw from later on. The radicalization of people largely drawn from wellness circles has perpetuated long-standing stigma around body size, destroying all nuance in the process. Yes, yoga can help you become healthier, and yes, obesity is a risk factor for negative health outcomes. But yoga (or any wellness practice) will never make you immortal, nor will shaming someone for their current health ever result in a magical transformation.

Ironically, the ancient texts modern yogis love to quote from are rooted in contradiction and nuance. They regularly warn against binary thought. Such a skill is damn near impossible when algorithms reward the presentation of opinion as fact and performative justice juices follower counts. Still, philosophy is what first drew me to yoga. Algorithms aside, abiding by the nuances of this pursuit has always been challenging.

The entire philosophical project of Advaita Vedanta is a critique of the assumption that reality divides cleanly into self/other, subject/object, real/unreal. Maya, often translated in a pedestrian fashion as "illusion," is considered the cognitive habit of mistaking provisional, constructed categories for ultimate reality. In this light, maya is essential binary perception. Patanjali's Yoga Sutras warn against the tendency to sort experience into fixed, opposing categories, particularly identifying the self with the body/mind complex versus pure awareness, which is a binary that the whole practice is designed to dissolve. In the most popular modern text, the Bhagavad Gita, Krishna repeatedly warns Arjuna against what he calls *dvandva*, "pairs of opposites." He instructs the archer to cultivate equanimity (*samatvam*) to transcend pairs entirely, which he frames as a prerequisite for clear action, not a retreat from the world.

This is not modern yoga, with its flashy postures and binary thought. The yoga that trickled down in America beginning in the early 19th century was qualitatively different. It had to be, given how far from the Iron Age we were. Ancient messages can resonate, though they were recontextualized for a Western audience. Over the next two centuries, waves of Indian gurus sailed and then flew to America to bring "authentic" yoga to Americans, some with good intent, others cognizant of the financial implications. The pursuit remained largely philosophical throughout the 19th century. Then, with the emergence of new, rigorous forms of yoga emerging in India in the early 20th century, spiritual hopefuls in New York and California dedicated themselves to a postural practice designed to yoke spirit to matter. As it became more woven into the fabric of American society, acolytes transformed the practice. Fine, everything evolves. But the binaries (*You must be vegan! Your health is your fault!*) took over.

This is the lineage my practice is descended from, with all the grace and beauty as well as cultural baggage. American yoga was designed for and sold to white, middle- and upper-class citizens. Over time, as physical yoga captured the cultural psyche, yoga was categorized with other holistic practices from foreign lands. A medical aspect was attached to it. Yoga became a panacea for the body's physical and psychic ailments, marketed to accomplish amazing feats, including curing cancer, a replacement for antidepressants, and a phenomenal weight loss tool. A direct line can be traced from small ashrams to conspiritual social media feeds.

The medical benefits weren't a huge draw for me, though I certainly bought into some of them. My pursuit was largely physical. I wanted to drop into splits and press into hand-stands like the strong yogis next to me. I briefly flirted with a handless headstand to mimic Dharma. I eventually accepted my limits. I had to, given how much my career started depending on yoga.

9

Here's the situation I found myself in a year-plus into teaching yoga.

I'm employed at a few small studios when an opportunity comes up. One of my teachers recommended me to a manager at Equinox, a former family-operated chain of gyms launched in New York City in 1991 and sold to a private equity firm in 2000. The company had national ambitions in 2004, though each location still felt local. Nice, clean, a place for strivers in fitness and life. The gym model Equinox launched: you want to shower, hang out there, meet up with friends for a class and then bite after.

The financial side is appealing. No yoga studio pays an hourly rate; none offer health benefits. Equinox does both. At the time, I'm cobbling together enough $20 yoga classes to pay my rent in Jersey City. I also spin at a Wednesday night party in the Lower East Side called Kollektiv alongside DJ and tabla player, Karsh Kale. The success of that party at Kush gives me a little cushion, though with a catch: the club is shutting down soon. I'm in full hustle mode.

The manager takes my class, then informs me that I still need to audition at the club. I'm no fan of group auditions. Weird environment. Performative. You're in a room with people you're competing against. How are you really going to judge anyone based on three minutes of instruction?

I show up at the cattle call on a Saturday afternoon along with roughly 50 other instructors. A group of managers sit in the front with clipboards. I'm aggravated before we even begin. They're looking for a vibe, not proficiency, not integrity. They want actors, not instructors. I move through the random series of disjointed poses for nearly two hours before I'm called to the front, one of the last chosen. By this point, I'm over it.

I know I'm about to blow my chance but I don't care. I step up, put everyone in a squat, then mention the email Equinox sent us, which said something about light movement. I cracked a joke about how I shouldn't have worked out earlier. The yogis laugh; the managers sit stone faced. I teach a complex arm balance series and walk off. Over half the instructors can't do it, but I was being a dick, not to them, but kinda to them. I never get a call.

A month later, the first manager reaches out. Despite club protocols she wants me at Equinox. Her boss is moving to Chicago tomorrow, so she had him sign off on my hiring paperwork. He was in such a rush he didn't pay attention to the cattle call list. I'm hired.

For the next 16 years I'll teach thousands of classes in New York City and Los Angeles for the club. I'll travel to nearly every location to lead my signature program, Flow Play, a yoga and music program I developed with Philip Steir. I'll lead three yoga teacher training programs alongside Stephanie Culen, graduating dozens of new instructors. And I'll evolve beyond yoga to teach studio cycling, kettlebells, ViPR, HIIT, strength training, and a few other modalities. My friends jokingly call me Mr Equinox.

The managers who ignored me during the cattle call will all become friends, though I'm not sure they remember me from that afternoon. That doesn't matter. What does: remembering life is never a straight line.

Equinox teaches me a lot about life. One lesson: spaces we deem "spiritual" are rarely the ones where actual growth happens.

10

The early debate was studio versus gym. Studio yoga (preferably with a lineage) was pure. Gym yoga, spiritually debaucherous. No way you're going to achieve enlightenment when the sounds of members clomping on treadmills and dropping weights are just feet away. Never mind that the indie studio is situated above a boutique chocolate store, it's the perception that matters.

A ridiculous debate. Before Equinox, I'm teaching at two spots in Hoboken. A small studio promoting body positivity over spiritual cosplay, which I appreciate. The other is the YMCA. I lead fun classes with incredible people in a low-ceilinged, old-carpeted basement room. Members show up in sweats and baggy tees, not overpriced Lululemons. No ego in that room, a far cry from the holy oneupmanship I witness in supposedly pure studios across the river. Get me into a gym, stat. It's where I'm most comfortable.

Equinox has received some flack for its price. Yet at the time, Jivamukti cost $250/month. For that, you get unlimited classes and the privilege of paying $15 for a vegan smoothie. And a bathroom where you're supposed to "let it mellow when yellow," meaning don't flush urine to save water. (The public health department made them remove those signs.) There's one shower in the Jivamukti bathroom. The spigot is intentionally stuck on cold so no one cleans themselves for too long. Capitalism pretending to be conservationism.

You pay for what you desire. If your goal is absorption into a yoga discipline, an independent studio is worth the investment. I've always been more of a movement syncretist, so a gym with diverse offerings is a better fit. The debate about where to practice is more indicative of a territory claim than it is a quest for purity. Most Equinox instructors also teach at yoga studios. I was one of them until my schedule hit 20 classes a week. Plus, Equinox deducted taxes and offered health benefits. Independent studios didn't have the infrastructure for that. Spiritual feeding only goes so far when you're starving materially.

Take Atmananda Yoga, where I became certified in 2003. Students from that time will painfully recall allegations of sexual abuse aimed at the founder, another all-too-common trend in yoga communities. I'm not surprised to discover that Jeffrey Epstein spent a lot of time at this studio years later. Records show he spent thousands of dollars a day there. I'm not sure how that's even possible.

Atmananda's six-month teacher training program requires weekly "karma yoga," a cute term for free labor. Everyone must work shifts at the front desk, clean the studio between classes, and teach (without pay) even though we're not actually certified yet. Their program costs $2,500 per student. With 30 in my cohort, that's $75,000. Yet no one is being paid to manage operations because we're all rotating shifts.

Near the end of our program, the founder sits us down in a circle. All minus one, the woman who dropped out after alleging that said founder rubbed ice in inappropriate places while giving her a "free" massage (and which might explain the Epstein connection). Founder is sitting next to his girl-friend, who helps run the studio. Starts telling us all about the allegations, which pivots into him claiming he can't help himself when it comes to sex. He just wants to have it all the time, with a lot of different women. His girlfriend is silent. A good time to mention the gender disparity in the program: 28 women, two men. Nothing comfortable about this scene.

The situation actually gets worse. Founder holds up a stack of envelopes. Unpaid bills. Rent, electricity, who knows what else. He's playing victim as I'm doing math. The space is on Broadway between Prince and Spring. Prime SoHo real estate. But you're telling people who've paid you thousands of dollars that you can't manage money. Yet you want to be treated as a spiritual guru. We leave the meeting in a haze. Are we even going to get our certifications? Will they matter given the growing scandal around the founder's self-admitted desires?

To answer: we do, and the scandal doesn't hold us back given he's a bit player in the larger yoga landscape. Not to downplay his damage. He's just no Bikram Choudhury or Yogi Bhajan. A separate point: spirituality is sometimes presented as separate from economics, as if the power of soul vibes transcends silly things like paying rent or employees. An argument often made by people who don't have to worry about things like paying rent or employees.

A deeply held philosophical conviction is one thing. Financially struggling people hold spiritual beliefs, but survival comes first in the hierarchy of needs. The American spiritual landscape, and the wellness community it birthed, is often dominated by people at the top of the pyramid. Easy to claim money is irrelevant when you have plenty of it.

That's the studio I trained in. Not unique that the founder had issues; it's not like yoga inherently transforms you into something you're not. If anything, spiritual practices have the potential to bring out more of your bad qualities. Though the opposite is true as well. From my experiences, most small studios are run by earnest, hard-working people who believe in what they teach.

I find the same qualities at Equinox. Despite popular opinion, not only wealthy people join. Teaching there throughout the 2008 financial crisis proved that. Many people in New York City lost their jobs; one of the clubs I taught at was on Wall St, directly across from the stock exchange. A number of members (public school employees and administrative assistants, not hedge fund managers) were in financial straits. Many kept their memberships because it offered relief from the stresses of life. Some people value their daily sweat and will do what they can to keep it accessible.

Equinox had other assets that helped shape my career and understanding of movement. The club helped craft the group fitness model. Most gyms offer two, maybe four classes a day. Equinox offers dozens across all movement modalities. While more common now, no other gym was investing so heavily in programming back then. A boon to members, and to me: my movement program greatly expanded thanks to all the classes I took and, eventually, taught. Those modalities also deepened my relationship with yoga. Movement is a conversation.

I miss that investment as much as my colleagues and managers. From my experiences, most people teach yoga with great intentions. They deliver for their students while fulfilling a personal desire to earn a living by moving people.

Equinox is largely known thanks to their marketing efforts, which is where it gets dicier. The chain was early in promoting inclusion, be it DEI or LGBTQ+ issues. They featured models actually representative of the spectrum of people who worked at and attended the clubs. They were also early on in promoting marijuana legalization, devoting an entire campaign cycle to it. I taught the first "activated" classes in Los Angeles, where a local supplier gave every student a free vape before we started. They were fabulous.

Being image-forward has drawbacks. While campaign models were of every color and sexual and gender orientation, a common trait persisted: they were all ripped. Body inclusivity never found its way into ad campaigns, a shame given that a percentage of their clientele was not represented. This decision reflects the changing nature of the company, however. A few years into my tenure, the board experienced a shake-up. Fashion industry veterans were installed, replacing fitness professionals. Marketing got sharper while the club's emphasis on group fitness lagged. Equinox bought SoulCycle in 2011 because, in part, the club was falling behind in that modality. A lot of old school instructors weren't happy about handlebar pushups and two-pound weights making their way into cycling studios. Sometimes, fusing workouts in creative ways adds value. In this case, extra movements detract from the mechanics and integrity of cycling. But they sure make for good photo shoots, which is where the club chose to place their energy.

Equinox was ahead in the renaissance of gym culture imagery, transforming the Venice Beach Gold's Gym aesthetics of the seventies into a chic lifestyle brand. Many other fitness and wellness brands followed. When Instagram launched in 2010, an entire nation of hopefuls were ready to curate their own versions of this phenomenon. Consciously or not, the Equinox image proliferated across platforms. This is when wellness became an industry.

11

Be careful about the spaces you hang out in. They will inevitably transform you, and not always for the better.

Watching the explosion of wellness products in America certainly caught me off guard given my "wellness journey" was defined by cobbling together rent money while hustling all over New York City and North Jersey.

Shri Yoga was an Anusara studio that consumed 5,000 square feet in Tribeca. The intention behind the studio was right; the economics, not so much. Many mornings I was assaulted by winds whipping from the Hudson River as I trudged across the empty parking lots of Exchange Place in Jersey City. A sigh of relief as I peeled back the door to descend to the PATH train, located on a dock above the river. A few minutes later, I reemerged under what remained of the World Trade Center, lunging up subway stairs, again assaulted as I walked north on Hudson Street. Unlock Shri's large sliding door by 6:45 am to prepare for no one to show up.

Making a living as a yoga instructor is no easy feat. Not now, and definitely not in 2004. Some studios expected you to show up a half-hour early and stay after class to field questions and "build community" without pay. Exploitation masquerading as spiritual development is all too common.

For the record, Shri was the opposite of that. The owners paid a fair class price even when no one showed up. Other studios couldn't claim the same.

One perk of the hustle is free workshops. Sally Kempton, an old school teacher who lived in an ashram for 30 years, led a meditation workshop at Shri. During a Q&A, someone asked how long she stays *there*, that magical place where thoughts cease to exist, pure silence, total absorption. She laughed. Two, maybe three seconds. An audible gasp filled the room. This woman has dedicated her life to this practice and the longest she experiences cessation of the churning of mind stuff is…two seconds? What's the use, really?

A weight was lifted from my shoulders. Many myths circulate about yoga, one being the goal of meditation is to stop thinking. More like turning a flood into a trickle. Brains create thoughts. One of their many jobs, and one they're not known for turning off. Cultivating an ability to yoke the stream of thoughts to a single focus is a more apt description, which is where Kempton lands. You're not going to completely silence those neurons. You do have control over how loud they are. Meditation is volume control.

And it's really hard. Let's not leave that out. From college through today, meditation has been a recurring practice in my life, which I've only been able to stick with for a few months at a time. In my deepest yoga days, I could get in a solid hour straight, though that was a stretch. These days, it's more like 10 minutes, usually when I'm frazzled. Many books and teachers tout the benefits of a daily, committed practice. I believe them. My friend Neil has put in an hour of zazen every day since the mid-seventies. He claims it helps him cope with his anxious mind. I imagine such a practice would help many of us.

For me, the greatest benefit is nervous system regulation. My body slowly softens as I deepen awareness of my breathing. It goes something like this: the first 5 minutes are generally excuses as to why I should be doing a dozen other things. My home office has a couch, stationary bike, and small area for stretching and yoga, so I tend to spend most of my time here. Probably not best to meditate a few feet from my computer, but it's also my sanctuary. I improvise. That challenge works its way into my meditation.

Dharma Mittra used to say it's easy to meditate alone on a mountaintop. Try doing it in the middle of New York City. He chose to live in that city *because* of the challenge. Electric pricks washing over my skin as I settle into my seat *is* meditation.

Settle I do. Sometimes it only takes a minute. Sometimes, eight minutes in and I'm all over the fucking place. A sweet spot eventually emerges, where my mind is fully trained on my breathing, the main focus of my practice. Some people choose a mantra; some, an image. For me, the feeling of my breath has always been the focus that draws me in deepest. After years of panic attacks stealing my oxygen, sitting on a mat and intentionally breathing felt like taking my physiology back. A mechanical, respiratory rebellion.

Meditation plus time equals results. When I sat longer, I felt more ecstatic. Sometimes. Other times it's still torture. That's how I landed on a 10-minute practice. Someone once told me to end it while it's still good. If you hate sitting and drag the session out, you won't return. A while back, I built myself up to 20 minutes, then noticed not wanting to meditate at all. Challenge is good, provided you're up for it. If you start avoiding it altogether, forcing it isn't the best idea.

So the best I can say about meditation is that it defrazzles me a bit. Instead of an onslaught of thoughts rushing at me from every direction, I sit calmly to reflect on what's most important in that moment. Just like bodies change with age, there may be more to it at some point. Regardless, the benefit I've discovered from a (somewhat) regular practice is already enough.

As with yoga, there's no one way to meditate. Certain external focuses and trappings that I discovered early in my yoga practice threw me off. Chanting for global veganism, but also the belief that meditation brings about world peace. While sources for this claim are numerous, the Dalai Lama talks about cultivating inner peace as the only feasible pathway to global calm. Not a bad idea, cultivating inner peace, though a bit simplistic. Have you ever met *people*? A whole bunch of them don't care about such goals, a feeling I fear is endemic to some portion of our population. I won't hold my breath for world peace via breathing with your eyes closed, so it's good that meditation isn't about breath retention (though some styles incorporate it).

A few ways to look at this. If meditation brings about inner peace so that I, the meditator, become a more peaceful person, I'll carry that energy into the world. I'm less likely to cause chaos or choose violence. I can get down with such a notion. Certain instructors took it a step further, as they always do. Their claim was that us, a group of 20 or 30 yogis seated in the East Village of one of the most expensive islands in the world, could bring about world peace through the content of our mind stuff. That we could heal Tibetans, for example, whose country has been at risk of colonization for generations. No amount of white people energy in Manhattan is going to force the CCP to overturn their longtime desire for land exploitation. It's such a simplistic and stupid idea writing it down pains me. Yet this belief was currency in the wellness space at the time and, to varying degrees, likely still is.

A hard reality to square. Most people show up to the mat for good reasons. Then the grift takes over. Those honest intentions get co-opted because yoga influencers believe themselves capable of unrealistic things, all the while refusing to engage in civic activities like voting. They believe spiritual practices transcend silly earthly problems. The riddle at the heart of this issue is never addressed: Tibet (to continue with this example) will only be freed through political power, yet the yogis of Manhattan pretend politics is irrelevant. Or perhaps their thought powers will somehow invade the less durable consciousness of CCP leaders and force their hand. These things always get fuzzy, quickly, when you apply logic to them—one reason I've encountered yogis who swear logic traps you in dualism while their expertise in feeling rises above all that. Despite their wildest wishes, politics is not a vibe, man.

Politics affects everything around us. If you can't see that, you're likely not negatively affected by them. Or you are and don't realize the origins of your discontent. Either way, brushing aside political realities in pursuit of spiritual ambitions is not doing anyone good, except perhaps yourself. Which is fine if that's your aim. Just don't pretend you're contributing to societal good by bypassing political realities.

Vibes matter, sure. But they don't negotiate with biology. All the "right thinking" in the world won't stop cells from mutating or chronic disease from manifesting. You can sit in a Manhattan yoga studio manifesting world peace until your knees ache, convincing yourself you're in total control of the universe. Then the universe decides to remind you who's actually in charge.

"I DID MY OWN RESEARCH"

12

Never a good sign when the doctor asks if you're sitting down.

I already knew. My testicle was as hard as a rock. Not a lot else it could've been. She confirms testicular cancer. I take it as well as I can, given what I discovered over the weekend: men that suffer from cryptorchidism (an undescended testicle) during youth are much more likely to develop testicular cancer. My right testicle remained lodged up there until I was seven. Three rounds of hormone shots (long needles puncturing my ass) are hard to forget. Thankfully they worked. I didn't need surgery to provoke the ball to drop. Plus, my mom took me to Toys R Us for a new GI Joe after each shot.

I'm guessing doctors in the eighties didn't know about the increased cancer risk. I certainly didn't until I started doomscrolling. My oncologist tells me the cancer had been forming for months, maybe years. I'm lucky it hadn't metastasized. Surgery is obvious. She wants two rounds of preventive chemotherapy. I agree, though I quit after the first. I "did my own research." Instead of YouTube, I read medical journals and learned another round would decrease my chances of remission by only one percent. I was already well above 90% thanks to surgery. The first round kicked in a few more points. That round, for three days, was rough (with apologies to people who go through many more). My oncologist tells me she's satisfied with my decision.

Here's the thing about medicine: it advances. Mortality rates for testicular cancer were 90% in 1900. In 1982, when I received hormone therapy, mortality had dropped to 20%. By 2014, the year cancer struck, it's well under 1%. As much as people complain about the limits of medicine, we should take stock of our good fortune as well.

The procedure also changed. Historically, a testicle was removed through the scrotum, a painful process that requires months of healing. Today it's plucked out through the groin. A much easier healing process, provided you don't offend the stitches. I was back in the gym performing light workouts three days after surgery. I taught classes that day as well, albeit without demonstrations. I waited four days after chemotherapy to return to teaching. Big mistake. Too exhausted to properly teach, I struggled that day. Probably me trying to prove to myself I could roll through cancer with no issues, not respecting the body's healing process.

In the wellness world, cancer isn't just a process; it's a metaphor. Wellness influencers are obsessed due to its pervasiveness. This obsession produces wild assumptions, like pretending cancer attacks from without, not within. Environmental conditions and lifestyle decisions certainly influence the mutation of cells. But if there's anything natural to humans, it's cancer, which is better described as a process than a disease. Over 200 types fall under the umbrella term "cancer."

Having lost friends to cancer, I read Siddhartha Mukherjee's *Emperor of All Maladies: A Biography of Cancer* shortly after its publication in 2010. The physician and biologist is one of the most lucid science writers around. Cancer, he notes, isn't an aberration, a glitch in the matrix of the human experience.

Rather, cancer cells are mutated, distorted versions of the cells that make us us. The disease process begins with a single mutation, which can then unleash malignant growth. Built into our genome, cancer seeks immortality in the same way we do. "They are more perfect versions of ourselves," he writes, because they grow and adapt faster than normal cells. Great for the process of cancer. Not so much for us.

This is why a "cure for cancer" is a bit of a misnomer, albeit not impossible. A cure for "a form of cancer" is more reasonable. Rapid developments in mRNA-based vaccines train immune systems in specific ways that could stop the growth process. I don't want to completely write off the possibility of defeating cancer outright. Targeted therapeutics designed for individual bodies are closer on the timeline. Great news, though considering how expensive precision medicine is, such interventions will not be widely available for some time.

Mukherjee isn't the first writer to tackle this dizzying domain. In her book-length essay, "Illness as Metaphor," Susan Sontag warns against cancer metaphors. Because people generally don't understand its etiology, cancer is labelled mysterious and capricious. Language describing cancer is often militarized: you go to war with it. Sontag notes that repressed emotions and incorrect thinking are sometimes thought to result in cancer, tropes that proliferate in wellness circles. The blame falls onto the victim, who apparently didn't live a pure enough lifestyle.

Sontag writes that psychological explanations for diseases like cancer provide a sense of control over experiences over which we generally have little of. Such psychologizing acts as "sublimated spiritualism," a secular means of affirming the primacy of spirit over matter. When a biological process is treated as a psychological concept, we're better able to come to terms with it. The problem is that psychologizing often obscures or denies the reality of the disease.

Sontag argues that this entire system of relating specific

emotions to specific diseases is a hallmark of thinking about diseases whose causation is not well understood. Near the end of her essay, she writes the cancer metaphor "will be made obsolete, I would predict, long before the problems it has reflected so vividly will be resolved." She believes we'll abandon the metaphor once cure rates improve. She also realizes we'll apply these metaphors elsewhere, which is exactly what happened at the onset of Covid-19.

Psychologizing disease is nearly as ancient as cancer. Hippocrates associated cancer with black bile, the humor whose accumulation was said to cause melancholic disorders, such as depression. Think about that: the father of medicine devised a system in which all health phenomena were distilled into four categories; one of them formed a relationship between cancer and depression (along with other fun stuff, like sexual dysfunction, ulcers, and diarrhea). When wellness influencers pop into your feed claiming cancer is caused by bad thinking, remember this lineage stretches back millennia.

Hippocrates wasn't selling celery juice cleanses or guided meditations, however. The wellness cancer grift is real. A range of so-called detoxification supplements made from apricot kernels, black salve, or "functional" mushrooms are on sale somewhere on your social media feed. Clean eating diets are huge. Essential oils are pitched as killing cancer cells (they can't) and ozone machines are marketed to treat cancer (they don't). Even Nobel Prize winner Linus Pauling got sucked into pseudoscience, claiming that megadosing Vitamin C staves off the disease (it doesn't). Anti-vax contrarians have followed in his wake, certain that ivermectin is the next cancer miracle cure (it isn't, at least based on currently available data).

While these purported cures and treatments sound ridiculous on paper, we can't discount their power when you receive a cancer diagnosis. I was quite susceptible to the influence of the LA yoga scene when diagnosed. Just down the block from the Marina del Rey Equinox is American Botanical Pharmacy, which isn't actually a pharmacy but a supplements shop owned by herbalist Richard Schulze. The man has repeatedly been contacted by the FDA for claiming his products have therapeutic effects without clinical evidence. The word "cancer" appears eight times in the 2018 FDA letter, four years after I bought one of Schulze's supplemental smoothie blends that tasted awful and didn't do anything for me.

As with most "warning letters" sent by that toothless agency, the store remains open and his online business is functional. To this day you'll see "Your Body Can Create Miracles! It Just Needs Your Help!," followed by a link to a derivation of the blend I purchased. Little ever changes, including the magical thinking that drivers wellness folk into marketing magical cures that only benefit their bottom line. The irony is, for pointing out this grift, I'm the one accused of being a sellout.

13

By far, the biggest criticism I've received in six years of *Conspirituality* is that I'm shilling for Big Pharma. How could I possibly support an industry that has harmed so many people? I give one of two responses, depending on my mood. First: Big Pharma, send those checks! Surviving as a writer is no easy feat. I need all the help I can get, and you haven't given me shit!

The honest answer: there's a world of difference between pharmaceuticals (the product) and executives focused on shareholder value. Those lines get blurred when companies knowingly pump opioids into society to get the population hooked. In a deregulation-obsessed nation like America, every industry gets overtaken by capitalistic fervor. Big Pharma, yes. Big Wellness as well.

No exploitative company should be let off the hook. Some

pharmaceutical companies, and the insurance and hospital systems they compete with, certainly exploit us. Yet trashing evidence-based medicine is a major currency in wellness, which makes the type of criticism I offer challenging. I'm not cheerleading for millionaire executives exploiting the system. Hundreds of thousands of Americans file for medical bankruptcy every year due to medical bills. Then there are those who can afford the basics but are regularly stretched thin when needing help (the camp I fall in). I've lost two friends to cancer because they couldn't afford insurance, only discovering the diagnosis when it was too late. Fucking tragic.

There's another side. There's always another side.

If I was diagnosed with testicular cancer in 1814 I wouldn't be long for this world. Since it happened in 2014, my treatment was quick and relatively painless. Because I had good insurance, out-of-pocket costs for office visits, surgery, and chemo amounted to a relatively mild $3,000 (compared to the $15,000 it would have cost).

Yet even that sentence is painful. Why out-of-pocket charges exist in one of the wealthiest nations in the world is baffling. My wife and I currently pay $800 a month for health insurance, and that's through her employer, which picks up most of the tab. We're hit with co-pays nearly every time we visit a doctor. Because she has dense breast tissue (like roughly half the women in the world), any screenings beyond a basic mammogram cost extra. Oh, this is fun: basic mammograms often fail to detect problems in women with dense breast tissue. Every year we have to consult our budget to see if we can only cover the basics or pay thousands for all the tests. For many Americans, the latter isn't even an option. Some years, it's not an option for us.

Wellness influencers often reduce the healthcare system to a binary, which doesn't reflect the scope of the problem. Evidence-based medicine is breathtakingly fascinating and the system it's trapped inside can be outright deadly. Wellness practices can provide actual healing while also being outright misleading and, at its most extreme, equally deadly. I've interviewed dozens of people who've lost family members because they chose meditation retreats and juice cleanses over oncology. The solution to a broken healthcare system isn't selling false hope. Sadly, people turn to charlatans because they have nowhere else to go. Influencers are ready to exploit their vulnerable positions.

I'm not debunking wellness misinformation here like I often do on the podcast, however. What interests me are the false promises spun up in wellness spaces, coupled with an incessant idea that some perfect form of health is waiting for all of us. While part of wellness marketing is focused on healing you from disease, the lion's share is dedicated to making you feel better than better. You know, optimizing and biohacking. Ironically, these cottage industries can lead you astray from actually being healthy.

The potential harm really hit me while working on a 10-month investigation for the *NY Times* about the marketing pipeline created by MAHA's top influencers, many of whom graduated from being Covid contrarians and supplements salespeople to working in the administration. We identified dozens of key influencers, then fed roughly 12,000 of their videos and podcasts into an AI system, asking a list of questions. The system spit back thousands of transcript snippets, which we spent months poring over in order to identify patterns in their language and approach. Collectively, these media were listened to over three billion times. Not small accounts with little reach. They're an integral part of a movement that values individual health over collective health.

Disparaging expertise is an essential tactic in their playbook. We found hundreds of examples of influencers relating Covid measures to Nazi Germany, telling listeners not to trust doctors while claiming there are no reliable vaccines. These influencers regularly called the American healthcare system a "sick care system." They claimed the system intentionally harms patients. The 18-minute video we published in August

2025 barely scratches the surface of what we reviewed (though tells the broader story and reveals their tactics quite well).

MAHA influencers avoid talking about the politics of health, however. They often pretend health transcends politics or is completely unrelated from social realities. Then they weaponize data about chronic diseases, which predominantly affect low-income and minority groups, in order to sell products and services to people who can afford them, further widening the gap in healthcare outcomes. With Kennedy lording over our public health system, handing out leadership positions to fellow anti-vax activists and free market champions, we're learning in real-time just how political health actually is.

I know the wellness mindset well because I lived it through various occupations. As a consumer seeking to heal my ailments, I paid for many wellness interventions, like homeopathy and acupuncture, which were marketed as cures to my problems. None helped. I avoided toxins they told me to fear, refused impure foods that would supposedly damage my health, and was rewarded with an eating disorder that hijacked a massive chunk of my adult life.

To this day I'll vouch for many practices within wellness spaces. But some of them, boy, watch out. The grift is so baked into the infrastructure that it helps to step back and figure out what we're actually talking about before we go any deeper.

14

"Wellness industry" is a bit of a misnomer. Rather, it's a variety of industries catering to the umbrella concept of "wellness," a term that's also rather ambiguous. According to the Global Wellness Institute (GWI), this industry is valued at $6.3 trillion, with projections of reaching $9 trillion by 2028. They break it down into numerous subcategories: mental wellness, personalized medicine, wellness tourism, traditional and complementary medicine, and physical activity. Categories already too vast to quantify, likely including figures that far exceed the scope of the definition. Makes sense given they're a nonprofit with a vested interest in spreading the gospel of wellness. The consulting group, McKinsey, puts the figure at a more sobering (but still valuable) $2 trillion, ironically more valuable than the global pharmaceutical industry that many wellness influencers rage against.

Back to a definition: GWI defines wellness as "the active pursuit of activities, choices and lifestyles that lead to a state of holistic health." The Wellness Alliance, a member-driven group that partners with companies, describes it as "an active process through which people become aware of, and make choices toward, a more successful existence." The World Health Organization, which is more concerned with public health outcomes than lobbying for specific businesses, defines wellness as "the optimal state of health of individuals and groups."

Vague definitions that don't necessarily push the conversation forward. An optimal state of health looks different from individual to individual. Group health, which is essential if you want to better understand dynamics that inform personal health, doesn't reflect the ambitions of the individual.

Likewise, "holistic health" is unclear. The term is often weaponized by wellness influencers, usually at the expense of "traditional" medicine. Many top influencers use terms like traditional, conventional, evidence-based, Western, and allopathic as slurs. They pretend evidence-based medicine is only interested in baseline health, like not being sick. Yet the WHO defines health as "a state of complete physical, mental, and social well-being and not merely the absence of disease or infirmity (illness)."

While this definition aligns with the aforementioned

descriptions of wellness, the two industries are often placed at odds. Influencers position their products and services in opposition to traditional medicine, often spreading misinformation in the process. There's nothing wrong with having "influence" over people by sharing workout videos, guided meditations, and the many other domains that fall under the term. That changes when you misinform about clinical research or pretend science supports wellness products, which most often it does not.

Still, it's easy to understand why wellness's influence has grown. Even the greatest offenders of scientific illiteracy are correct that there are good reasons to distrust the American healthcare system. An insidious triangle of competing industries (the hospital system, insurance agencies, and pharmaceutical companies) has screwed us over for a century. We're the only industrialized nation in the world without socialized medicine. My entire life, I've listened to politicians from both major parties pontificate over why we supposedly don't want universal healthcare. Polls consistently show the opposite. No wonder wellness brands try to fill a gap with a posture of care and the confidence of used car salesmen. The landscape isn't exactly hard to exploit.

Yet it's unfair to claim doctors, nurses, and researchers aren't interested in preventive medicine or wellness. Many popular influencers pit their services against medical professionals, who they claim are all bought by Big Pharma. Ironic, given influencers aren't accountable to anyone. By law doctors have to disclose financial relationships with pharmaceutical companies. No such reporting exists for influencers.

15

Social media levelled the playing field for ambitious influencers. You no longer needed an agent to book a photo shoot to get your image into the public eye. Or to sell products and services. Gone were the days you needed a publisher to put your words into the world, factcheckers be damned. I take no issue with advocating for yourself; I've built a career doing it. But when people pretend to perform journalism without the rigors of journalistic standards, or to offer health advice without the training required to do so, we should be wary.

Unfortunately, social media platforms flattened our understanding of health and science. No longer confined to yoga studio banter, misinformation rapidly spread across the globe. With all the world's information at everyone's fingertips, many in the burgeoning wellness industry believed themselves capable of assessing science without the required critical thinking skills. They frame themselves as true critical thinkers, claiming anyone advocating for "conventional" medicine must be paid to do so.

High-profile visibility of wellness practices might be new, but the concepts at the foundation of wellness are not. If anything, being old is a badge of honor. Ayurveda views health as a harmonious convergence of body, mind, and spirit, a theme that informed early yoga. Though Traditional Chinese Medicine wouldn't be coined until the mid-20th century as part of Chairman Mao's global propaganda project, the system's folk medicines are roughly as old as Ayurveda. Ancient Greek and Roman civilizations partook in proto-wellness trends like public baths, exercise regimes, and dietary guidelines. They also believed illness to result from aberrations in lifestyle and environment.

As globalization set in due to evolving communications and mobility technologies, syncretistic spiritual philosophies and alternative medicine movements proliferated. The 18th and 19th centuries saw an emphasis on "natural" healing as a reaction to the growing influence of chemistry, anatomy, and physiology. Thus you get homeopathy, osteopathy, chiropractic, and naturopathy, each claiming to offer "true healing." Tagging along is New Thought and Christian Science emphasizing the role of mental and spiritual fitness in physical health.

While the term "wellness" first appeared in the 1650s to define "a state of good health," modern usage took a few centuries to root. John Harvey Kellogg blended exercise, nutrition, and spiritual belief, as well as the bland cereal he believed would cure men of the sin of masturbation. An entire movement strove to make wellness synonymous with moral virtue, self-improvement, and the pursuit of vitality through natural means. Kellogg championed "clean living" through diet and movement. Like today's influencers, he often played loose with science to sell his ideas, and products.

Literal snake oil salesmen, chiropractors, naturopaths, osteopaths, and the like battled the growing field of medicine throughout the 19th century. They did pretty well considering medicine was in disarray. There were no national standards for graduating doctors. Since education was for-profit, university mills were established. Get 'em in and out as quickly as possible. If a program took four years, a nearby college offered a medical degree in three. The free market was alive and unwell when it came to science education during this time. Confusion about who could be a doctor and where and how they were allowed to practice provided a huge hole for alternative medicine practitioners to run through.

I can't blame people for seeking help outside of the medical establishment. Infections and wounds were frequently treated with amputation. Bone saws earned their name. Anesthesia hadn't been discovered yet, so you got a shot of whiskey and a towel to bite while the doctor hacked off your forearm. Or maybe they stuck a few leeches on the cut, because that was wildly popular. Constipated? Here's a mercury pill. Just don't stick your genitals in new places or your solution to a sexually-transmitted disease will be arsenic.

Treatments for autistic people were horrifying. And yes, autism existed in the 19th century, and well before, despite what modern anti-vaxxers claim. Doctors were convinced hydrotherapy (holding patients underwater until they lose consciousness) does the trick. Another tactic: spinning patients in a chair until they pass out. Yup, that thing children do when testing the boundaries of gravity was top-tier medical treatment. Tobacco smoke enemas were in favor. If I were alive 200 years ago, some enterprising professional might stick a spiked iron rod into my abdomen to treat my hernia, then shove a chain up my anus to cut off the blood supply to my hemorrhoids. I'd probably believe some dude selling alcohol as a tonic, too.

Order was finally imposed on this chaos in 1910. Abraham Flexner's report revolutionized medical and higher education in the United States and Canada. After founding a progressive college-preparatory school in Kentucky, he was commissioned to evaluate medical schools across North America. His report exposed poor standards and profit-driven motives of many institutions, sparking sweeping reforms that transformed medicine into a science-based, university-affiliated profession. His report also forced many schools to consolidate or close. One tragic legacy is that these were often in low-income and minority regions, meaning these citizens' healthcare options were further limited.

Alternative medicine practitioners faced a choice: acquiesce to this consolidation and prove your approach works or good luck out there. A number of osteopaths and reform chiropractors choose the former. Homeopaths and naturopaths generally went with the latter, forcing most to close shop (for a while). Healthcare moved into the fledgling hospital system as doctors banded together to offer their services under one roof. Businesses took notice, instituting the late 19th-century practice of paying bulk for employees to attend hospitals for primary care. The insurance industry was born from this relationship.

Not that everything was kumbaya. Doctors were cutthroat. Insurance agencies quickly grew greedy, driving a wedge between practitioners and the young pharmaceutical industry. The innumerable problems Americans experience with for-profit healthcare today stem from this tension. By mid-century cracks in the system were already visible. Citizens wanted something more personal, more personable. They felt unseen, unheard. Growing distrust of medical orthodoxy, partly spurred by the counterculture movement, helped wellness become a commodity. Within a few years consumers embraced organic food and yoga alongside acupuncture, chiropractic, and herbal remedies.

In the 1950s, biostatistician Halbert Dunn introduced "high-level wellness," differentiating wellness from mere absence of illness. He defined it as an "integrated method of functioning which is oriented toward maximizing the potential of which the individual is capable." Though an uncommon name in wellness circles, Dunn's sentiment is often repeated. The notions of biohacking your biology and optimizing your life are direct descendants of his work.

In fact, you can hear echoes of Dunn throughout the MAHA landscape. In his 1973 book, *High-Level Wellness*, Dunn cites the WHO definition of health as more than just being free from sickness. He then wonders aloud why "doctors and nurses and health workers so frequently forget the meaning of this definition?" Dunn offers no data on the medical system; just vibes. He then proclaims what wellness actually is: "There are times when you are fairly alive with the glow of good health—with wellness. Alive clear to the tips of your fingers. You have energy to burn. You tingle with vitality. At times like these, the world is a glorious place!"

Dunn seems to be describing flow states. A runner's high. I've certainly felt in flow after a basketball game or at the top of a rigorous climb on my bicycle. Of course, such a feeling isn't limited to cardiovascular endurance. Yoga and meditation have put me in this place. I agree with Dunn: it *is* a glorious place. Yet he seems to conflate health with a particular physiological reaction. Such conflation is common in wellness writ large: the notion we should perpetually exist in a state of flow. While certainly wonderful, health is better regarded as a state of homeostasis. Not where we're just not sick, but also not an otherworldly, psychedelic state. A "trip" is only worthwhile because you return. If you were perpetually tripping, *that* would be the status quo. Nothing special. No lessons for your normal state because normal *is* psychedelic. Who knows, maybe sobriety would be the goal.

While Dunn promises high-level wellness has its own "life" and "bang" without any concern of a hangover, his definition becomes oddly pedestrian. Being in this state "requires that the individual maintain a continuum of balance and purposeful direction within the environment in which he is functioning." I appreciate his recognition of the importance of environmental factors, though a "continuum of balance" implies the very homeostasis that defines good health. He then distinguishes between a medical definition of health and a wellness one: his system calls for maximizing health. Complete health, he says, is a static ideal. He'd rather you maximize your body by directing progress "toward an ever-higher potential of functioning."

Unlike the anti-establishment rhetoric weaponized by wellness influencers today, Dunn is a fan of public health and medications. He might define his concept in opposition to a perceived doctor's visit but he also recognizes the importance of evidence-based medicine. The impulse is understandable: the call to not just survive but thrive is inspiring. While my struggles with food and exercise as it pertains to self-image were crippling, I truly love weightlifting and cycling and yoga and hiking because of the feelings I have during and after workouts. I don't feel like merely getting by. Better feels possible.

As a self-help protocol, Dunn's book fits perfectly coming out of the sixties. As a self-help manual, fine, but things get murky when he turns to science. In "The Cellular Commonwealth" we witness a rift between inspiration and misinformation. The chapter reads like a proto-influencer guidebook. Dunn is in awe of the "hundred trillion cells" in the human body. He goes on: "It would actually take about 37 thousand worlds of the type that we have, each one with about the same number of people in it as our world has now, to equal the total number of cells in the body." He uses this absolutely useless image to argue for a personal government over the unruly chaos of bureaucracy.

Dunn quickly butchers physics by mashing it with biology. He invokes gravitational fields before declaring humans are subject to innumerable "energy fields" inside the body and out. What does that mean? Irrelevant. Sounds mystical. Cells organize into different systems, he declares, like cities joining a nation-state. A benevolent ruler is necessary if we don't want the spirit of the body to die due to the resulting chaos of a cellular authoritarian. "We need to respect the cells. We need to take their dissatisfaction to heart."

Dunn's dualism is apparent when he references the "I" somewhere inside our bodies, but who knows where, exactly? While more reserved than loud, his health advice is regularly doused with mysticism. Yet the entire chapter can be boiled down to the most mundane advice imaginable: eat good food and move regularly.

That's the thing about the wellness industry: basic advice doesn't sell books. Umph is needed. Well enough is never enough when the limitless potential of product sales sit on the horizon. And that constant upselling of miracles trickles all the way down to the studio floor, where fitness instructors are expected to be healers.

16

At times, the role of healer was thrust on me. The most common questions I receive involve medical issues. Students recovering from an injury who have to modify their practice. Offering modifications is within my scope of practice. Then there's "this is happening, what do you think it is?" type queries. I always respond the same: that's a great question for your doctor. I might suggest poses to avoid, leaving it up to their discretion. Sometimes, I refer them to massage therapists. People generally know when they're pushing it in a fitness environment; adults deserve respect for their agency. Diagnosing medical conditions was certainly not part of my yoga teacher training, however. It's not part of anyone's yoga teacher training, though that doesn't stop instructors from making all sorts of bold claims.

I've heard way too much speculation and outright misinformation presented as facts in yoga spaces. Mostly about nutrition. Instructors present their dietary choices as ideal for everyone. They speak freely about "toxins" without having a clue what that term means. And it's not limited to food. Every medical condition is apparently subject to the miraculous resolve of our psychology in yoga rhetoric. We can supposedly cure ourselves of cancer, depression, anxiety, the gamut of health problems with the right attitude. All sorts of malaises dissolve when properly tuned to the universe. Then I never even need to see a doctor. Provided I keep paying for their classes, workshops, and retreats.

The wellness sleight of hand: fear that, buy this. Reading Dunn's work, I don't get any sense he's selling untested products. He's part of the sixties counterculture that wanted to combine everything and prove synchronicity between fields, an ethos that provides a direct line to the type of thinking that occurs in modern wellness spaces.

Much of my college education involved reading literature from Dunn's era. Beyond classroom reading, I was interested in a particular community of syncretists: Joseph Campbell, Mircea Eliade, Arthur Koestler, Alan Watts. The latter, a profound alcoholic and eloquent rhetorician, would often hop on stage drunk out of his mind to deliver elegant sermons. As with today's wellness folk, he offered a galaxy-brained perspective. In *Does It Matter?*, he writes, "The concepts of health and sickness, good and evil, better and worse, have the same use and relation to life as those of long and short, high and low to carpentry: even a short piece of wood can be three inches long. Even cancer is called a growth, and when Ramana Maharshi was dying of cancer he resisted the doctors, saying, 'It wants to grow, too. Let it.' This is, perhaps, an extreme example of renunciation—not of love or energy—but of willing right as against wrong, and thus of renouncing one's own separateness from everything that happens, which is what Tillich called 'the courage to be.'"

Watts correctly identified anxiety as a potential trigger for negative outcomes, though he often viewed health as spiritual, not biological. Wellness influencers continue that trend, albeit from a predominantly Christian perspective; the convergence of anti-vax wellness rhetoric with Christianity is a phenomenon deserving of its own book. While Watts briefly served as an Episcopalian minister, his curiosity about Buddhism and Taoism caused him to flee that profession. Alongside other beat-era syncretists, he sometimes applied a whimsical notion of balancing forces as essential to health. Today's wellness acolytes are more interested in a muscular Christian approach. MAHA's health "war" is a "spiritual battle." Prayer, submission, and surrender are prescribed as medicine, a bulwark against the satanic forces of chemistry and industry.

Koestler also reverberates through the generations. No fan of reductionism, he advocated for a holistic approach in biology and psychology, calling humans "holons," integrated parts of a larger environment that cannot be reduced to single entities. There's much to glean from his insights, predominantly his emphasis on the role of the environment in health. Unlike today's influencers, however, he was a fan of pharmacology, believing it could radically alter the health of society. Koestler hoped science and ethics would converge to protect against the dangers of totalitarian excess, which makes sense for a Hungarian Jew who fled Britain at the beginning of World War II. He also championed dignity in death. Diagnosed with terminal leukemia in 1979, he and his wife, Cynthia, committed joint suicide in 1983.

Joseph Campbell and Mircea Eliade, two figures responsible for shaping and defining the field of comparative religion I was immersed in at Rutgers, saw health and healing as spiritual journeys. For Campbell, good health provided a means for transformation and integration, far more important than biological states. Eliade, who devoted much of his career to the study of shamanism, saw healing and disease as deeply entwined with the spiritual and symbolic dimensions of existence. He too viewed this as more relevant than material processes. Shamanic traveling provided tools for psychological and spiritual healing. While neither man was explicitly hostile toward modern medicine, both felt its reductionist focus on biology denied the mythic and symbolic dimensions of health.

Campbell believed Western medicine and modern culture suffered from a crisis of meaning, neglecting mythic aspects essential for true healing. He lamented the lack of spiritual integration and the tendency to focus solely on physiological cures. Eliade wrote extensively about the desacralization caused by Western medicine, claiming it "demystifies" illness by reducing it to biological processes. He argued that illness, in many cultures, was regarded as a sacred ordeal. Healing required a restoration of cosmic order, not just the removal of symptoms. Both argued for an integration of science with myth, ritual, and the symbolic imagination, rather than relying solely on clinical paradigms.

I navigated this tension between spiritualized healing and medical science throughout college, long before wellness was *that* culturally influential. These thinkers were correct that the environment plays a primary role in individual health, something we know today thanks to the social determinants of health. But this isn't what midcentury syncretists were referencing, just as it's not what wellness influencers mean when espousing terrain theory, the outdated idea that germs don't cause disease. Both support a form of metaphysics of disease.

Biology and physiology matter more than those syncretists allow. Sure, the environment can trigger illness. Sometimes you just can't avoid a virus. Sometimes, your genes are going to hijack your health no matter what. Beware anyone flattening health to a single cause.

Still, syncretist insights into the emotional and communal aspects of healing remain relevant to this day. A positive attitude has beneficial health effects. The issue is that modern influencers vastly underestimate the terrifying power of nature and overestimate our place within it. They deflect when their philosophy brushes up against the brutal indifference of the world. In their retelling, nature is only there for our well-being, much like a religious believer treats their god.

17

I didn't have the luxury of that theology. When cancer hit, I needed coverage, not nature.

Facing testicular cancer and knee surgery 11 months apart, my health insurance through Equinox thankfully covered the lion's share of expenses. As mentioned, I initially split my time teaching at independent studios and Equinox. In many ways reflective of my life overall, split between wellness practices and evidence-based medicine.

Your environment changes you. At first, I'm surrounded by people interested in deepening their yoga practice. Once hired at Equinox, many of my students turned out to be doctors, nurses, and healthcare workers. They appreciated that I remained within my lanes of movement and anatomy. The same students grew frustrated with instructors stepping outside their scope of practice. I'm sure if I spent a decade-plus in college, medical school, and residency only to listen to someone spout pseudoscientific nonsense, I'd be pretty pissed. I too shake my head when hearing "you know more about your body than a doctor" while trying to decompress in a yoga class. I'm sure it's triply painful for doctors.

Of course we're capable of knowing our bodies. One of my favorite concepts is proprioception, your ability to know how your body moves through space. An innate sense, you can increase your ability to recognize subtle fluctuations through awareness practices and physical workouts. While most everyone has a general sense of this skill, specialized receptors can be fine-tuned with practice. Which is why I'm comfortable moving through space in a yoga class; I've put in decades on the mat. Those skills don't translate to soccer, where I'd be lost matched against someone who's spent decades in that space.

Most of us can know our bodies well. But there's unconscious processes we know nothing about, many of which we have no control over. People indoctrinated into wellness culture sometimes assume we can gain control over these processes. There are a few documented cases of yogis using breath work and meditation to control physiological processes, like heartbeat and blood pressure. The value of such exercises on the nervous system are worth exploring. Claims go off the rails when it comes to disease prevention. This is what I mean by a metaphysics of disease: the notion that you can stave off innumerable illnesses through mind set, breathing, and nutrition. Wellness practices can certainly help your health, but let's not trick ourselves into magical thinking.

Whole foods and regular movement are key for achieving a positive health profile. Such recommendations are considered boring in industries that regularly pump out products that have to seem unique, new, and "science-backed." Practitioners make outrageous claims in order to stand out. Inevitably, talk turns to "natural," as if living like cavemen will return us to a state of optimal health.

In 1903, British philosopher GE Moore coined the term "naturalistic fallacy" in his book, *Principia Ethica*. He argued against defining moral qualities like "goodness" solely based on natural properties, such as pleasure or anything that occurs in nature. This framework is important for understanding wellness's predatory practices, which tug on the belief that humans have an innate superiority over other biological life, and are therefore not bound by its rules. They claim we cannot possibly be harmed by nature, a position that can only be held from a place of deep privilege.

Alan Watts might have viewed health a bit too holistically, but he kept the brakes on when considering our place on this planet. In *The Book*, he writes, "We do not 'come into' this world; we come out of it, as leaves from a tree." A lot of folks think we descended here from on high, immune from the innumerable challenges biological life faces. The irony is our success as a species is largely due to public health measures wellness influencers often decry. They claim immune systems are fortified through nutrition and exercise; nothing produced pharmaceutically tops that.

The onset of a wide-scale, concerted effort to deny humans of vaccines, as evidenced by the ascension of the MAHA movement, is the clearest proof possible that we're victims of our own success.

Naturalism hyperbole fails when confronted by data. The most common causes of death throughout the 19th century included tuberculosis, cholera, measles, smallpox, typhoid fever, and diphtheria. Wonder why none of these make the list today? We're far more likely to be stricken with chronic illness than an infectious disease, which is its own problem. Just not the problem anti-vaxxers are claiming to solve, especially when many infectious diseases can lead to chronic disease. We're also far more likely to live to old age. Life expectancy was 46-48 years in 1900. Vaccines are partially responsible for the extra 30 years we've gained.

Wellness influencers paint an irreconcilable picture. They market a back-to-the-land ethos, a time before humans were corrupted by industrialization. By their logic, we should all be harvesting our own food and living from the land. Yet they also enjoy technological conveniences considered basic now: refrigeration, indoor climate control, transportation, the internet. They're fine with globalized supply chains when it suits them, in their own lives and for the products they monetize. They're fine with chemistry provided it gives the appearance of being natural, turning a blind eye to the countless industrial processes behind the foods and products they use and sell.

For a certain subset, one I saw up close while living in Los Angeles, testosterone replacement therapy, Botox, and cosmetic surgeries are perfectly acceptable. Fine, you do you. When the same people claim vaccines, seed oils, and food dyes are "toxic," the story changes. Their claims about nature crumble under scrutiny. I'm not pretending to be contradiction-free. I hope, at least, I pause long enough to think through my beliefs to ensure I'm not being this blatant of an asshole.

Highways aren't natural. Neither is indoor plumbing or thermometers. Cars are definitely not natural, nor are the phones influencers type out naturalistic fallacies on. Most every facet of an influencer's life has nothing to do with the "nature" they picture when marketing organic produce or beef tallow. They ignore the manufacturing processes producing that produce, the slaughterhouses churning out that beef, the supply chain delivering the products to their grocery store. So many "unnatural" technologies afford them the privilege of shitting on things they don't understand.

Speaking of ignorance, consider an ingredient wellness influencers regularly rage against: petroleum. On its face, influencers should love this "natural" substance. It hits all their buzzwords: it's ancient, consisting of plankton and algae, common ingredients in their superfoods and supplements. Thanks to MAHA, petroleum is pure evil due to its use in manufacturing food dyes. Kennedy's associates label them "petroleum-based food dyes" as a slur, as if anyone eating ultraprocessed foods are huffing oil.

I treat chemical slurs like any other: I want to know the reference point. In this case, petroleum serves as the raw material from which key chemical building blocks are derived. The manufacturing process of food dyes involves multiple steps that transform petroleum into vibrant colors. First, petroleum is distilled to isolate specific compounds suitable for dye production. These compounds go through complex chemical reactions like sulfonation, nitration, and azo coupling. They're then purified through filtration and refinement that removes contaminants. The resulting dye contains zero petroleum.

If you're not into foods containing food dyes and can afford to not eat ultraprocessed foods, wonderful. It's best not to eat too many of these types of foods. Influencers claim dyes are neurotoxic, which is true, but at levels far higher than what's allowed in our food supply. Food dyes aren't the reason ultraprocessed foods are unhealthy, but wellness influencers have capitalized on MAHA's propaganda to score moral points.

Here's what gets me about this: many influencers, including those closest to Kennedy, sell supplements manufactured via the same exact petroleum process. Synthetic vitamins are more stable, more reliable, and cheaper to produce. Nearly every time I hear an influencer scream about food dyes, I visit their website, scan their products, and quickly identify petroleum-based supplements. They're not even trying to hide it. Just look at the product labels. If you see Vitamin A in the form of retinyl acetate, Vitamin B2 as riboflavin, Vitamin B9 as folic acid, or Vitamin C as ascorbic acid, your supplement began life as petroleum.

The hypocrisy is astounding. Easily checkable, they bank on their followers never doing the math.

Sadly, they're often correct.

18

Logic doesn't stand a chance against dogma.

Wellness, at its extremes, becomes a form of religion: it promises a return to ancient ways, romanticizing a time when untainted foods were yanked from soil and butchered by clean hands. A little dirt never hurt nobody. Eat those microbes and steel your immune system! Optimal health was guaranteed because our ancestors never fell ill. The Bible is often misquoted to support coffee enemas and ancient Indian techniques are apparently filled with urine drinking immortals. Things get Freudian quickly. All our holes become opportunities for monetization through junk science rooted in a faux historical imaginarium.

Everything was pristine, once, organic, pure. How we were meant to live, unadulterated, wild, in communion with earth. Glorious bread, the wheat of life, thrives in this fictional past. Celiac disease is for the impure. There were no allergies, back then. Raw milk suckled from a fertile cow, drained down your gullet. Feasting like cavemen staves off all illness. Glowing skin and radiant health are yours for the manifesting when tallow is slathered across your surfaces. The imaginarium intoxicates at every turn.

Assembled from nostalgia and marketing, ancient humans weren't gleefully humming along in thriving communes. Their diets were shaped by geography, drought, conflict, whatever wild animal was slow enough to be caught or roots were forageable. The premise of pure ancient food is a product of modern privilege. It's easy to imagine backwards, provided you never experience what our ancestors actually endured.

Wellness influencers lean heavily into the myth of ideal food because it sells not only products but an identity. To eat like the ancients is to resist modernity's poisons. The complexity of agricultural systems, supply chains, and production methods dissipate when blame points to gluten, sugar, nightshades, tainted water from an impure spring. The solutions sold in wellnesstopia to address them (parasite cleanses, beef tallow, supplements) create more problems than they solve. Oddly, the more obscure influencers make the ritual, the more authentic they deem it to be.

Archaeology reveals a starker picture. Ancient Egyptians feasted on bread loaded with grit; their dental records show it sanded down their molars. Medieval stews nearly floated in salt to keep them from rotting. Romans drank adulterated wine; resin and lead were common ingredients. Most people alive before the Industrial Revolution were closer to starving than thriving. Meals weren't so much curated as endured.

Wellness orthodoxy erases that context, cherrypicking "good" food from ancient iconography. An ideal marketing move: cleanly eat your way through the stresses and alienation of modern society. Sell escape, a narrative, a powder that offers better than better. Buried underneath the glossy sheen lurks a deeper neurosis. The pursuit of purity can fuel disordered eating and cycles of shame for failing to live up to image-driven ideals.

Which is why influencers must avoid discussion of the social determinants of health. They need to paint a picture of equity even as they sell products for the privileged. Actual toxicity *is* a problem for people living in industrial neighborhoods or under flight paths; for immigrants picking and processing "pure" foods for poverty wages; for those living in food deserts, in educational deserts, in healthcare deserts.

Seed oils don't cause chronic disease. Working full-time and not being able to afford healthcare might.

The wellness industry is rooted in predominantly white middle- and upper-class communities. Their understanding of space is defined by the place they inhabit, which became increasingly the case when trapped in our phones during Covid-19. We were all caught off-guard. There hadn't been a global pandemic in a century. Many cities made the same exact poor decisions (and experienced the same exact poor results) during Covid-19 as the influenza pandemic of 1919. Public health protocols around masking, isolation, and tracking were left up to cities, which implemented wildly different courses of action (or none at all).

The wellness community treated Covid-19 as a personal sleight. They raged against public health guidance as a violation of individual liberties. They framed themselves as experts, claiming researchers and scientists were all in cahoots against us. They promoted (and often monetized) all sorts of quack cures. They defaulted to "natural is better" rhetoric, claiming supplements can cure what vaccines cannot. They fled Los Angeles for Austin, banding together in tight-knit groups defined by contrarian identities. They immediately rejected whatever expert advice trickled in. And when they were struck with Covid-19 themselves, they claimed it was a "created" disease bioengineered to do maximum harm. One influencer blamed the severity of his infection on eating a single bite of chocolate. He said this while seated in a portable red-light sauna that he just knew was helping cure him.

Covid-19 broke a lot of brains. Having spent decades in wellness, I realized instructors who had implored me that "I'm my own best doctor" actually believed it. And I understood we were going to be poorer as a society because of it.

But to comprehend why people retreated into their own isolated bubbles during a crisis, you have to understand how the environment shapes us. You have to consider geography.

GEOGRAPHY OF A TRIP

19

A color-coded map of New Jersey defines my home state by vibes: *pretends to be New York, pretends to be Philly, Alabama, Pineys*. Natives can guess each region. I grew up in *Diversity*, both true and laughably false. True: the section includes Black hoods in New Brunswick and Newark, heavily South Asian Edison, heavily Judaic East Brunswick. False: I grew up in a one-square-mile, ultra-white borough called Milltown. As with the cities I'll live in as an adult, diversity abounds, though within segregated regions.

The mill was no longer functional by the time my family arrived in 1976, a vestige from a 19th-century Goodyear tire factory. Born in Beachwood, a shore suburb across from the infamous *Jersey Shore* town of Seaside Heights, we moved when I was one. The borough planned on transforming the run-down mill into mixed-use residences and studios. Instead they tore down the entire structure. The grounds remain rubble nearly 30 years later, which is how things move in suburbia: slowly, if at all. Explains why Milltown voted for Trump three times: it's the type of place where lifers yearn for a past that never existed, where bravado and volume defeats nuance and context. By 18, I needed to get the fuck out. I secured a dorm room at Rutgers even though I could have easily commuted.

Milltown is a sleeper, figuratively and literally. When researchers developed meprobamate, they named it after my town due to the tranquil feeling you get while there. Miltown (Wallace Laboratories inexplicably removed an "l" from its name) sedated millions of adults throughout the fifties. The first billion-dollar drug in history was adored by Hollywood. Stars shilled for the pharma blockbuster. Milton Berle earned the nickname "Uncle Miltown." In 1960 Wallace was sued for monopolizing the tranquilizer market back when America still honored trust laws. Five years later Miltown was reclassified as a sedative. Another five passed before it became a controlled substance. People woke up to the fact that this little helper had created addiction and dependence all along.

Every animal is a product of its environment. Milltown offered all the conveniences and trappings of small town America. State politicians regularly pointed to our burb as an ideal community representing the best of middle class life. Underneath the tranquil veneer slept a racist community that, like so many others, wasn't climbing the ranks so much as treading for survival.

Mobility existed, for a while. My maternal grandparents owned a trailer park on a highway in East Brunswick that somehow provided for eight children. My paternal grandparents resided in their two-bedroom house for over 50 years in an even sleepier borough, South River. My Pop Pop worked a variety of menial jobs while Nanny was employed in a sweatshop stitching clothing for her entire career. My lineage is filled with disgruntled, angry Eastern Europeans who fled Hungary, Poland, and Russia to get hustled into mediocrity and abuse in Jersey as laborers and heavy drinkers. Their situations were, from my understanding, vastly improved from where they came.

My parents escaped some of that. They worked career jobs

and now live relatively stable lives on pensions, a luxury I will never know. Instead of companies providing lifelong safety nets for dedicated employees, we bet our retirements on the whims of the stock market. Some employers even "match" a tiny percentage of your gambling money.

Instead of becoming a salaryman (as the Japanese phrase it), I pursued other avenues of work and existence, guided mostly through an enduring love for music and literature. After working at the Discovery Channel for two years, I vowed to never work in another cubicle again. So far, I've been successful, though hustling for decades isn't romantic. Still, my mind craved a different space. I knew it wouldn't be found in that place, 45 hours a week stuck in a drab midtown Manhattan office building.

In his book, *Space and Place: The Perspective of Experience,* geography professor Yi-Fun Tuan distinguishes *place*, which he describes as security, and *space*, freedom. We're attached to a place while yearning for a space. A push-pull that's defined my life. I can't escape the Jersey in me. Age grants wisdom, or at least acceptance. Still I desire the freedom to move as freely as possible, not only through physical space but imagination as well. A sudden change of place after high school created an opening to explore new space.

Tuan calls place an object with "geometric personality." Milltown might have appeared calm, but like the drug named after it, the interior was unsettled, always seeking escape into space, inevitably mired in inertia. Tuan notes that people suppress what they cannot express, which is why space matters: if you're limited in place, you'll likely be stuck in space. This idea is confirmed in my hometown: the whiteness of thought dominates the place. Without ever having visited, you likely know the space.

My 18-year-old self wasn't thinking about security, only freedom. So when the opportunity to get the fuck outta Milltown arose, I grabbed it for all it was worth, moving onto the grounds of Livingston College in Piscataway. Two towns over doesn't sound like a lot of distance, but it afforded me an entirely new sense of place along with a space I could never have dreamed possible. And the only way to truly understand a new space is to move through it.

20

In her ode to walking, *Wanderlust*, Rebecca Solnit writes, "Thinking is generally thought of as doing nothing in a production-oriented culture, and doing nothing is hard to do. It's best done by disguising it as doing something, and the something closest to doing nothing is walking."

Haruki Murakami has his own take on walking, the sped-up kind. In his memoir, he views existence through the lens of running, an exercise and meditation he credits with saving his life. As a jazz club owner, he regularly smoked and drank into the wee hours. His body never felt right. Not intent on a quick 5k, he took up ultramarathons. "I just run. I run in a void. I should put it the other way: I run in order to *acquire* a void." Likewise, Solnit calls walking "both means and end, travel and destination."

My love of walking comes from my father. He's spent a lifetime walking long distances, fast. Not running, just power walking without calling it that. No arms pumps or purposeful direction. His entire body pumps when engaging in this most natural bipedal activity. Even today, in his eighties, he outpaces me around his Las Vegas neighborhood. I'm six inches taller and 31 years younger yet struggle to keep up. To him, walking is more end than means; anxiety propels him as it fuels me. Walking, our shared passion, is an antidote to unnecessary fury, a means for processing life. The idea that you need to get somewhere quickly is embedded in my DNA. Hyperaware that I *should* slow down, I too often want to arrive fast. On my better days, slowing down serves as an ideal meditation. On other days, racing to the end triumphs.

My wife prefers the former me. So do I, when I can conjure him.

Walking is what I miss most about living in New York. No other American city comes close. Numerous rituals developed over my 12 years there. Here's one: I finished teaching my last class of the week at Equinox Tribeca on Friday afternoon. Out the door, grab a snack at Amish Market on the corner. Walk five miles home, over the Brooklyn Bridge, through Brooklyn Heights and Carroll Gardens and Gowanus, across the Union Street Bridge, sometimes Carroll St Bridge or 3rd St, to my Park Slope apartment. Another: on Tuesdays and Thursdays, I taught a 7:30 am class on 63rd and Lexington, followed by a 10 am class in Chelsea on 17th and 10th. Walk through Central Park to grab breakfast at Whole Foods in Columbus Circle. Most days I'd hop on the A/C/E to 14th, though on occasion I just kept my legs moving.

Whenever my father visits the city, we walk. One summer day, meandering through City Hall Park at the foot of the Brooklyn Bridge, I asked why he didn't raise me with religion. His answer is simple: he was raised with too much. Every Sunday, his parents forced him to attend the Russian Orthodox church in South River. They never joined. His dad was at the bar when it opened at 7 am. His mom, who knows. A whipping awaited my dad when he skipped (or when they found out he skipped). Soured him from religion for life. I don't blame him.

Besides music, walking is the closest thing to religion I've ever found. This connection isn't apparent when I arrive at Rutgers. The link between basic mobility and spirituality unfolds as I canvas New Brunswick's streets, usually with headphones pumping in A Tribe Called Quest and the Fugees, Stereolab and Radiohead from my Discman. At first, I had zero academic ambition. The closest discipline with any appeal is accounting. I served as class accountant for business classes in high school. Geometry and calculus confuse me; balance sheets are its own form of meditation. That career pathway quickly fizzled as I met new people and embarked on new experiences. And marijuana.

English seemed a more reasonable choice given my love of books. That trajectory didn't last long. African-American Literature, taught by the incomparable Ivan Van Sertima, is the best class I took at Rutgers. The man is a force of nature. Unlike other professors dumping six, eight books on us every semester, Van Sertima only assigns Ralph Ellison's *Invisible Man*. A chapter a week. I received my first paper back with a note: quit regurgitating information and think for yourself. C. I earned an A by semester's end upon realizing he's serious. He didn't want rote learning but the application of knowledge, which are very different things.

Van Sertima not only inspired my decision to major in English, but also to leave it. I soon learned that his class didn't qualify for an English degree, only toward African studies. I'm living on one of the most diverse college campuses in the country yet African-American Literature isn't considered studying English? That's not going to work.

Campus diversity helped grow my interest in numerous domains. Sports, for one. Most collegiate athletes are housed on Livingston; a number of training facilities are located there. Makes sense: the college was founded in the sixties, in part, to funnel minority students into one place. Every evening I'm in the campus gym playing basketball or volleyball with serious talent. Relationships built there translate onto campus grounds, which greatly expands my musical palate, political awareness, and spiritual understanding.

Like Thaxton, who handed me copies of the Dhammapada and Bhagavad Gita early in my first semester. A commuter from Plainfield, he ended up crashing on the floor of my dorm room the entire year. So did Vinny, a "sorta Rican" poet from North Bergen. Then there's my actual roommate, Calvin. I'm six-three and dude made me feel like a midget at six-seven, 400 pounds. Four 18-year old boys living in one small room for nine months is an education in itself. All readers, all aspiring philosophers of sorts, we made it work. Some tension, like the time Thaxton refused the floor and crammed next to me in my twin bed. Mostly laughter and dialogue. Thaxton believed my mind needed Eastern texts. I tore through both books, declaring religion my major the following year. Buddhism became the focus of my thesis and, in a lot of ways, my life.

Those two books aren't the only reason for my interest in religion. During the first semester of sophomore year, a friend sold me a bag of mushrooms. A week later, another gifted me a hit of LSD. For the next 15 months, psychedelics consumed me, reoriented me, propelled me in directions I never thought possible.

Let's start at the beginning. A group of new friends threw a seventies-themed party off campus. Pete and I arrived early. My high school crew started dabbling with marijuana in high school; I waited until college. Three of us five end up at Rutgers, which makes sense given our high school is roughly 20 minutes away. We quickly found our way into a creative community of artists and musicians, like the crew hosting the party that night. We turned off Easton onto Hamilton, walked up the stairs, knocked on the door. Abe led us into his bedroom, long curly locks hanging below bare nipples peeking out from denim overalls. We handed him a $20 bill, he returned a baggie with nearly an eighth of psilocybin-containing fungi. Have fun, he said. We quickly devoured them and returned to the living room.

I'm not sure how long they took to kick in. A pungent aroma of soil, a grimace chased by a swig of bottled water. What damage could that possibly do? Next thing I remember is swimming on a leather couch. Bill Withers crooning through the speakers. An incomprehensible lightness of being. Laughter, so much laughter, attached to a very specific and utterly foreign feeling: the complete cessation of pain.

Anxiety is like a sustained note playing in the background of my life. Here, I close my eyes. Bill transports me to an undiscovered world, his grandma's hands, kissing his love. I lean on him, or Pete, no matter. The everlasting note of stress perishes. Not fades, nor whimpers. The thing is gone.

Ironically, my great grandparents settled on Hamilton St when emigrating to America, roughly eight blocks from this party. My great aunt lives in the apartment that once housed an entire family in 1994, the year of my first exploration. Here I am, navigating new worlds as they once did, the psychedelic experience of settling in foreign territory after fleeing Hungary. My great grandmother never learned to speak English. New Brunswick, for a time, housed the largest Magyar population outside their homeland. Exploring a new land like that must have been quite a trip.

My trips won't all go as splendidly as the first. Some are existentially crippling. This evening, though, I glimpsed another way of experiencing life. We walked all evening, to the grease trucks, Voorhees Mall, the Raritan River. Many nights over the next year go like this, with friends, alone, brain plugged into headphones, bathed in starlight on cool New Brunswick nights. The cessation of pain no longer seems so foreign. My education occurs on these streets, in this state, walking.

The connection between the transcendent literature I'm studying and these states of ecstatic bliss clicks all at once. A pursuit I was built for.

21

Years before fake Buddha quotes proliferated on the internet, I was taken by the moral integrity of the Dhammapada, one of the most famous works of the Pali canon. The story of a young archer being tutored by a crafty godhead in another Indian text, the Bhagavad Gita, struck a different chord—metaphorical, metaphysical, exquisitely entertaining, even as the archer is being told to murder friends and family on the battlefield but hey, don't worry about, this reincarnated godhead told you it's all good. Arjuna isn't even the brother that achieves ultimate glory, but I didn't know that yet. Funny how his name is synonymous with victor now. At the time, I was too busy soaking in instructions. The entire text of the Mahabharata (the Bhagavad Gita is a section) will be read later.

Whereas the wild polytheism of Hindu literature set my imagination on fire, the simplicity of pedestrian Buddhism made more sense as a blueprint for existence. Buddhist metaphysics are all over the place. Heavens and hells and ghosts and gods. I never become a devout follower of any faith, Buddhist or otherwise. The four noble truths at the heart of the teaching stick with me, though. While skeptical of any overreaching "truth" about the world, this manual makes the most sense to me.

Let's go through them, with the caveat that I'm viewing this through the lens of secular American atheism. My senior thesis paper investigated how Buddhism is mistranslated when imported into America. Like many cultures, we have a bad habit of extrapolating current situations and rewriting backwards. We believe our ancestors were just us without the constant distraction of pocket computers. Setting the proper stage is important, as I'm not an originalist of anything, and my version of Buddhism is modern in every context. There's no possible way to know the "true meaning" of any ancient text, though we can certainly be inspired by them.

First, there's *dukkha*. Usually translated as suffering, I prefer (as do some translators) "dissatisfaction." Life doesn't always go your way. The reason: *samudaya*, desire or attachment to situations or outcomes. You want some shit to go down *this* way, but life curves and the thing happens *that* way. Don't worry, there's good news! *Nirodha*: you can stop craving and end suffering by relinquishing attachments. Which you do via *magga*, the Noble Eightfold Path. These interrelated practices shepherd you to nirvana: right view, right intention, right speech, right action, right livelihood, right effort, right mindfulness, right concentration.

The core lesson: become the observer observing the observed. Step back from expectations. Is the situation fucked up, or only what you hoped to achieve from it? Sometimes, it's really the situation. In this case, you do your best to detach emotional investment from it. Not *not* feeling, but fully feeling and moving through the situation with fortitude. Take the "I" out of it. It didn't happen *to* me, it just happened and I'm one of the people involved. That mindset shift helps alleviate the conspiracy of existence being *against* you.

More often than not, your expectations create suffering. So reframe the situation: it happened in a way I didn't desire or expect. I can either wallow in my misperception or open to the possibility that I'm not always going to get my way. Again, feel the loss, but move on.

One of the best antidotes to misperception is walking. I take all that frustration, sadness, rage, whatever is welling up inside and head outside. No goal. I just walk until I feel more at ease, then circle back home. Walking as meditation. Doesn't "solve" the problem, but offers enough space to distance myself from the situation. Clear my head. Let the cortisol surge dampen.

Another caveat: suffering is relative. Everyone can experience dissatisfaction, but perspective matters. Being born in a refugee camp in a war-torn nation is going to result in a whole lot of dissatisfaction impossible to understand if you're guaranteed a trust fund in Los Angeles. This isn't to say the latter person isn't capable of suffering. One thing I've noticed observing America's wellness industry, which often draws from Eastern aesthetics: underestimating your blessings often comes with the territory.

This happens individually and socially. My current study, the anti-vax community, reflects this habit. Without public health interventions like vaccines, antibiotics, and improved sanitation, many of us would not be here right now. We're privileged simply for being born at a certain historical juncture, beneficiaries of a quality of life that others never had an opportunity to experience. A privilege not spread evenly. As is human nature, the biggest benefactors have a terrible habit of thinking themselves oppressed. Strange phenomenon, though it explains the Trump administration's total disdain for critical race theory and DEI. Their political juice is squeezed from grievance, a motivator they'll never abandon.

Metaphysics also plays a role in the overestimation of ourselves. Another terrible habit: believing we're endowed with spiritual force instead of grappling with the evolutionary processes that resulted in, well, us. This habit often intersects with health. An entire subset of the wellness community thinks prayer, "correct" thinking (qualitatively different from the Buddhist prescription of right thinking), and a belief that we're spiritual beings (and so not subject to the biological laws other animals endure) are the true keys to health. While positive thinking plays a minor role in health outcomes, it won't replace vaccines when a virus strikes.

Retroactive spirituality is also in vogue: the belief that everything is "meant to happen" once the thing has already happened. We need to justify our beliefs to ourselves, though, and this is the quickest shortcut. Better to write it off to predeterminism than grapple with our expectations.

I appreciate the simplicity of secular Buddhist thought. No metaphysics to buy into, no baptism required, no declaration of faith demanded. Whether you consider the Night of Bodhi (when Buddha achieved enlightenment) metaphorical or real is irrelevant. In this rendering, enlightenment is never a final state. We're all going to fuck up. Enlightenment is a living, breathing commitment to keep noticing and keep trying to do better.

Plus, there's a roadmap. My mathematical neurosis lit up when discovering this equation.

A little backtracking. Shortly after learning to read, I created a system in which every letter of the alphabet is either positively or negatively valenced. That is, each letter sits on one side of zero. Add up letters into words, words into sentences, sentences into paragraphs, and every word, sentence, or paragraph is either positive, negative, or neutral. For years I tallied results on my hands, lifting and lowering fingers as I mentally spelled every word. Joy washed over me when a sentence turned out neutral, as that meant the meaning of the words was harmonious.

How was each letter assigned? No fucking clue. I can't remember how all this started, and the stultifying debacle ended when puberty began. The system just appeared in my brain one day. For years I followed it. Not all the time. A voracious reader, I rarely counted while devouring a book. It usually happened while in conversation, which made conversations difficult, or when alone thinking, which made thinking difficult. While ignorant of its origins, I'm confident this was my way of assigning order to the chaos of existence.

Which is similar to how religions develop: people observe patterns in the world and assign them meaning; that meaning becomes the lens for which they view (and judge) their concept of an ordered existence through. This might sound arbitrary, given the random appearance of a counting system in my young brain, yet when considering religious myths logically, you're likely to discover they're equally baffling. Plus, human brains invented all religions. They have to start somewhere.

Counting letters wasn't my only striving toward order. My mother used to drive to Shop-Rite in Hightstown to pick up groceries because that location always honored double coupons. I wandered the aisles while she filled the cart with whatever microwavable products my family would consume that week. I passed time by turning all the cans so that their labels were easily viewable. If some were misplaced, I would return them to their proper station. Even as an adult, I occasionally turn items if they're skewed, though not with the same veracity or agitation as when I was young.

I can invent all sorts of reasons for this behavior in reflection. As mentioned, there was some physical abuse in my home. I was bullied at school for being overweight and awkward. Maybe counting letters and fixing cans gave me some control in an otherwise unpredictable world. These habits calmed my racing mind, helped me focus on something within my grasp, even if that grasp was entirely of my own making. As Joseph Campbell would often say, we assign meaning to an otherwise incomprehensible universe. Not all assignments need to be religious. Sometimes, though, what begins as a pedestrian pursuit changes societies.

Which I'm going to guess happened to Buddha. He likely didn't suspect his legacy would last for thousands of years. In today's terms, he wasn't always a great dude. A deadbeat dad who disowned his family in his quest for enlightenment, he named his son Rahula, "impediment." Raising a child was a shackle that kept him from pursuing his goals. Later he instructed both wife and son, treating them as he would any other students. Rahula was the first monk ordained by his dad, so there's that, though it likely stems from appeasing his father as it was of his own ambition.

Still, Buddha was focused on founding monasteries, not world domination, even if he felt the philosophy he devised was universal in its application. His construction hit me hard because it provided a circular roadmap applicable to all areas of life. The eight directives, bundled into three categories (wisdom, ethical conduct, mental discipline), gave shape to my life. I could step back, consider my thoughts and actions, and weigh whether or not they lined up with what I considered to be a worthwhile pursuit.

Defining "right" has been a constant challenge in Buddhism specifically and religion broadly. This was the case in India during his time, in all the countries Buddhism was exported to, and in modern-day America. *Right view* traditionally meant understanding reality, a pretty broad directive. Buddha also discussed the law of karma, a concept that remains open for debate considering all the definitions floating around. Early texts simply define it as "action," yet a (likely unintended) metaphysics was injected into it. That's how we land on baristas telling you tipping is karma with the implication that if you fail to do so, well, then just understand why you get into a car accident leaving the cafe.

Right action, also a tough one. While a call for ethical behavior, a lot of people get caught up on the killing part. Does that extend to animals? Vegetarians argue yes, any murder is abhorrent, yet even Buddha directed adherents to never turn down a meal when offered by a host. Legend has it that Buddha died after eating rotten meat, which vegans might define as karma because that represents the reality they want to be the right one. Buddha would also define it as karma, though without all the moralizing.

It's all so tricky. Getting back to first principles, Buddhism offered me a general blueprint with room for interpretation. This led me to consider another relevant principle that helps me maintain some level of sanity: know what you can change, know what you cannot, know the difference between the two. If pain is caused by dissatisfaction, can I alleviate suffering by changing my actions, thought patterns, the vibe I currently inhabit? If not, no reason to get stuck. If so, do whatever possible to unstuck myself.

My study of Buddhism began while working as the religion columnist for Rutgers' newspaper, *The Daily Targum*, and covering politics and religion as a stringer for New Jersey's two major newspapers, *The Home News* and *The Star Ledger*. Part of my job involved interviewing leaders of campus religious organizations. A common theme quickly emerged: every person thought they had found the "right" religion. To be fair, this was on a spectrum. Some felt their path was one of many ways to find god, like tributaries spilling into an ocean. Others were more certain about their professed faith. All faiths are pliable, a fact applicable to the history of religions as well. They're also culturally dependent: Christianity feels wildly different in New Jersey than Ethiopia.

All of these factors swirled in my head as I studied, wrote, and reported on religion. They eventually led to my decision to become an atheist. It wasn't a long journey, considering I was, throughout my life, agnostic at best. The god I pleaded to while stuck in a body cast was more of an idea, a frustrated demand thought into ether. There was no adherence to scripture. I was picking it up as I went along.

One factor got me more interested in spirituality than anything else, though. And it was responsible for the closest run-in with theism I've ever had.

22

Many, most in fact, of my trips were fantastic. Not all of them, though. You heard about my first trip. There was another biggie.

A longstanding myth in left-of-center circles has it that psychedelics turn users progressive. The embrace of these substances by Silicon Valley executives and employees, a number of whom identify on a spectrum from libertarian to fascist, is enough to dispel this myth. The Silicon Valley of the late sixties and early seventies grew up with psychedelics, and they helped lay a blueprint for fascism and authoritarianism to follow today.

Psychiatrist Stanislav Grof put it best when calling psychedelics "non-specific amplifiers." They crank the volume on whatever's going on inside of the user. They don't magically insist the user adopt a foreign worldview. This isn't to deny the experiences of those who use psychedelics therapeutically. They've proven incredibly healing for me in certain regards, and have held up in early-stage clinical studies for alleviating depression, anxiety, PTSD, and suicidal ideation. But psychedelics have the ability to lead you to dark corners of your mind as well. Sometimes your mind is already dark and they're just saying, *while we're here, check this out*. Using totalizing language about psychedelics isn't helpful due to their immense range of possibilities.

Sometimes those dark spaces proved important to my personal growth. Sometimes a trip just sucked and I craved nothing more than falling asleep and putting the whole thing behind me, especially when I believed death was imminent or my mind wouldn't find its way back to baseline. Not every tragedy is a teachable moment. Or, perhaps more accurately, sometimes what you're taught is that you need to power through chaos and remember not to return.

November 1995, for example. An eight-gram mushroom comes into my possession. Sebastian arrives at my Somerset St apartment around 10:30 pm. We each eat four grams about 15 minutes later. At 11:15, we're walking past the hospital I'm currently employed at. Sebastian points at the emergency room and says, *I need to go in there*. I'm like, *my job?* I tell him that's a very bad idea. His friends agree to return to his dorm room and take care of him. Sebastian asks me to go as well. There's a problem: I'm meeting Jessica at the party we were supposed to attend. Cell phones won't be a thing for years. I'm not willing to ghost one of my closest friends. Despite Sebastian's protestations, we split up.

I let Jessica know something's speeding at me fast. We find the dance floor, immediately start moving. Some part of me dances outside of my body as "Superstition" dominates the room. Forty degrees outside and I'm sweating viciously. I realize I'm dancing directly next to an open coil heater. I realize I don't care. I'm back in that space where stress has evaporated.

We dance for, I don't know, hours? Eons? Ten minutes? We find a space to cool down and chat. I'm tripping hard, peaking in fact, but I'm there, with her, at least somewhat legible. I tell her about the situation with Sebastian. She asks if I want to visit him, then drives us to campus a few blocks away.

It doesn't go well. He's upset that we split apart, even after I explain while Jessica's sitting right next to us. His point of view makes sense yet I stick firm to my own. Logic is ineffective when emotions run high. Sadly, our friendship will never recover. Jessica drives me home. I hop out as she drives home.

Climb up to the third floor, turn right into Wayne's room. I tell him I'm tripping hard, too hard. He asks if I want to go over to Chrissie's. The crew is there smoking and listening to music. Instead of hearing what I should have—*hey dumbass, friends who know how to deal with bad trips are together and you can be with them*—I think, *more drugs?* No fucking way. I just want to play Sega Genesis and chill. He says cool, exits the room.

Turn on Crash Bandicoot, start playing. My eyes can't keep up. I keep dying, quickly. Crash pops up again for another game. I play again, die again. Then reborn. And die. And reborn. And, oh fuck, I need to turn this game off immediately.

I look at the clock. 1 am. The peak is just beginning.

Run into the bathroom, close the door, sit on the toilet to think through this, whatever this is. I'm losing concepts. I think of a word. My brain goes, *what is that?* Not just the word, the concept behind the word, the physical structure of it. If "chair" comes to mind, I question what one even looks like, what function it serves. I'm slipping fast when the next word pops up: *breathe.* The one I absolutely cannot forget. I'm cooked. Run out of the bathroom, into my bedroom, jump onto the mattress, slam the door behind.

Funny thing about that apartment: the heating broke constantly. Most of that winter is spent without any. Bonus: the window in my bedroom is slanted. Outdoor air always has access. I'm wrapped in two comforters, fully dressed in jeans, hoodie, socks, shivering. Another word I completely forgot: my name. I spent the next five hours trying to recall it. The first hints of grey peak through the dark window around 6 am. I remember my name and immediately fall asleep.

I don't recall all the thoughts racing through my mind during those five nameless hours. I'd love to wax poetic; it's just a blank. What I remember is the feeling. I'd been erased, I erased myself, trying to claw my way back to reality. I'm not sure what the qualifications for an existential crisis are, but I'm pretty sure this passed the test.

I realize this would put most folks off psychedelics for a considerable amount of time, like forever. I'm a gram under McKenna's "hero's dose" and that's just fine. Five might have ended me. The following Friday, I ingest a much smaller dose, just over a gram. Walk to Voorhees Mall, sit on the grass in front of the building where I'm taking Buddhism and Buddhist Art, music piping from a Discman, turn it off and meditate silently, the crisp sound of winter washing over me. A wonderful evening, alone with my thoughts. More importantly, comfortable with them.

Which is the reason I did it. Some people have told me their first trip was horrible so they never tried it again. Thankfully, my first experiences were incredible. Surrounded and supported by friends. When the first bad one rolls around, I know it doesn't have to be this way. That's why I reset my brain after such a harrowing experience. Remind myself that dose matters. I will never eat four grams again. A gram? That's my lane.

What I was learning then, though I hadn't developed the language for it, was the cessation of another longstanding human trait: dualism. As articulated by Rene Descartes, mind and body are treated as two fundamentally distinct substances. Meat animated by essence. Psychedelics dissolve this divide. Never before had I felt so inside my body yet separate from it. Usually, this is used to argue for dualism. At first, I felt the same. Over time, that veil disappeared.

Mental health and physical health are often said to complement one another. I find this distinction confusing. The brain creates the mind and controls motor movements. An entire field of science is dedicated to understanding how to alleviate depression (and other mental health maladies). Time and again exercise is shown to benefit such duress. (This is *not* to say it's all anyone needs, just that movement can help.) It made sense that the thing I wanted to do most when tripping was walk long distances. My mind and body were in sync. This felt a lot like the "union" I would later study in yoga.

As with yoga, mentors were necessary. Today, people often seek out guides for psychedelic experiences. Most of us broke college students weren't heading to the Amazon in the mid-nineties. So we tutored each other. A rite of passage. Experienced cosmonauts guiding curious friends. Like a game of telephone, you passed along the message. Always distorted by the end of the chain, but in this case the chain never ends, so the message is regularly remixed.

Brian played guide for our first psilocybin and LSD trips, the latter which I also did with Pete. He lived up to the moment. Kept us connected to reality while allowing our inner children to roam in awe. Pointed out cool shit. Fucked with our minds, gently. After roughly 20 trips, I started leading curious friends on their first expeditions. Not sure if this was the "right" way, but it's how it happened, and thankfully no disasters ever occurred. I've certainly heard about a few.

Given their ability to alter one's consciousness, the clinical study and therapeutic applications of psychedelics are potentially transformative. *And* I still support recreational use. I can't answer the question of who should take which route. I'm just aware that financial incentives tied to the therapeutic path should be included in the conversation, and that might not be the right path for everyone.

Bringing us to the collision between psychedelics and wellness. Living in the epicenter of this scene for 11 years, I watched yoga instructors in Los Angeles go from participating in their first ayahuasca ceremony to rebranding themselves as shamans in a matter of months. They quickly started charging for their services as "guides." I'm not anti-capitalist, but spiritual capitalism leaves a bad taste in my mouth.

If the story ended with yogi shamans selling retreat packages as a form of spiritual pursuit, I'd be annoyed but wouldn't criticize. It's the conflation between science and spirituality that raises my eyebrows. Endless yogi shamans discuss the medicinal benefits of psychedelics, a problem in wellness broadly. Sharing an anecdote about a transformational experience is a memoir. Imploring people to abandon anti-depressant medication because psychedelics work better is a scientific claim, one yogi shamans are unequipped to make. Yet a combination of personal experience and distrust of experts positions the influencer as a trustworthy source.

Distrusting experts is a longstanding tradition in America. When Richard Hofstadter gave the term form in his 1963 book, *Anti-intellectualism in American Life*, he was identifying a trend that's persisted since colonization. While his focus was business, education, politics, and religion, health and science have also been susceptible to this pattern. I've read numerous books about 19th-century medicine; wellness influencers would have been equally at home then. The intentional spreading of misinformation was a common tactic for chiropractors, osteopaths, and Heroic medicine practitioners. Believing you know more than people who dedicate their lives to a subject is a pastime in modern wellness. Sometimes a lucrative one.

I can empathize with people sharing their experiences with psychedelics on social media. My introduction occurred decades before these platforms arrived. If I had been born later, I too might have enthusiastically shared revelations given the profound impact these substances had on me. I just hope that I wouldn't have been susceptible to the sorts of pseudoscience presented as knowledge regularly being made.

Psychedelics led me to both a deeper wrestling with spirituality as well as an absolute fascination with science, considering what anxiety does to my body after graduating college.

Little did I know then, this transition thrust me forward in ways I never imagined possible, challenging many of the assumptions I had made about myself and the world beyond me.

23

The quickest way to challenge those assumptions was to change the scenery. One evening during my sophomore year, Alex and I dropped LSD at the East Brunswick Square Mall for some ungodly reason. As a movie theater employee, I was likely picking up a check. Shortly after ingesting, we were pulled over by a cop who saw two college kids and got a hard-on for provoking unnecessary anxiety. I had recently cut my hair short and was rocking a hoodie. Officer paid me no mind. Alex, long hair twisted into braids, wrapped in an oversized black trench coat, was pulled from the car and searched. He let us go with what he believed was a stern warning. The damage was done. That wallop of stress jump-started our trip. We were well on our way by the time we arrived in New Brunswick.

Voorhees Mall, my favorite part of campus. The most traditionally college-looking of all five campuses. Gorgeous brick buildings (and a few blandemic ones) surrounding a 28-acre tree-lined field. Alex and I meander down the slope. We stop to paint a mural—well, discuss the mural he would paint, as that was and remains his vocation—on the blank side of Scott Hall. Within moments, a voice floats behind us.

Peter is a history grad student working nights as a campus security guard. He starts talking about art before swerving to geography after finding out we live on Livingston. He tells us our campus was designed by a prison architect; administrators were planning on shuffling minority students to that campus. Those super-heavy, seemingly useless doors that connect the quads underground? Riot-proof protection. The school can lock them down at will. Besides, why else would a campus sit in the middle of an ecological preserve, two giant commuter parking lots flanking the sides? Visibility. The campus was built during the Civil Rights era. Pitched far enough away from town that police would arrive before anyone escaped. I'm tripping my face off and alarm bells are screaming, not because I'm worried that Peter is going to have us arrested (though I'm certain he knows what we're up to), but because I've tripped enough times on my campus to put the pieces together. I roamed those underground halls on acid and mushrooms and whatever else was around. Each time felt like prison. The cold drabness of the buildings makes sense.

We talked to Peter for two hours before returning to our… prison cells? I never trip again without thinking of this conversation, my isolated campus housing the majority of minority students. The space we occupy, which brings us to place.

The diversity of Livingston's student body is a refreshing change from Spotswood High School, where one black student, a transfer from the UK, graced the halls. Everything's different in Piscataway in 1993. Hip-hop is a shared language. Many of us congregate in the rec center to throw down on the basketball court. Segregation persists in the dining hall yet must be abandoned when locked in battle. The campus is a microcosm of the cities I'll later live in, the same patterns emerging 30 miles northeast in New York City. Neighborhoods clearly defined along racial lines though we all share a subway system. Friendships cut across lines, both in college and out. Exposure breaks boundaries. Livingston might be a suspiciously designed place, but the space is alive, fertile, fun. Educational. My degree is earned outside of the classroom, which both my life and GPA corroborate.

That space is not shared throughout America. I'm writing this chapter shortly after the murders of Renee Good and Alex Pretti by ICE agents terrorizing American citizens in Minneapolis. I've lived in four "shithole" cities (Jersey City,

Brooklyn, Los Angeles, Portland) since 1999. None are perfect. I've been robbed multiple times, thankfully never at gunpoint; break-ins, to my building or car. Crime happens with population density, whether out of necessity or sport. I fear the sort of theft rich men wage on our financial system far more than I've ever worried about walking down a city street. The illusions of place politicians weaponize relies on their voters' lack of understanding of space.

Sending the National Guard into blue cities has nothing to do with crime. The Trump administration knows that humans are easy marks when fear-mongering about place, however. An ancient story, though one many miss when directly living through it. The ever-present story of power. And power always demands more; never is enough enough. As for people who support such an agenda, one reason is lack of exposure: to other people, ideas, cultures, places. The reason my hometown repeatedly voted for Trump is because a lot of voters never left. They're so trapped in a monoculture they confuse their place with all of space.

Which we all do, to some degree. Yi-Fun Tuan pre-empts the MAGA mindset: "It is a characteristic of the symbol-making human species that its members can become passionately attached to places of enormous size, such as a nation-state, of which they can have only limited direct experience." My experience as well. America is too geographically vast to ever "get" it in full. While I'm grateful for living in cities, I have limited direct experience of much of American culture. I'm comfortable in a room full of ecstatic South Asians bouncing to qawwali in Queens but fuck it would be awkward witnessing one of those southern sorority TikTok dance-offs in person. One of those cultures genuinely frightens me. Yes, it's the one I'm ignorant of.

Still, I hold fast to the promise of what America represents. I have many, many problems with the hypocrisies expressed through white privilege, neoliberalism, and unfettered capitalism. I do my best to temper my frustrations with America's religious nationalism by remembering that this nation's call for equality is taken seriously by many of us, fractured and frustrating as the reality of that promise remains.

To wrap your head around that ambition (and the work needed to bring it to fruition), your place needs to be diverse. When your space reflects that ambition, even better.

Nature operates on the exact same principle: survival depends entirely on the diversity of the network.

24

Little wonder we received psilocybin shipments from Oregon at Rutgers. Little wonder that I end up living there.

Oregon is home to the largest mycelium network in the world. The 8,000-year-old *Armillaria ostoyae* spans three-and-a-half square miles and weighs an estimated 35,000 tons. Located in the Malheur National Forest in eastern Oregon, the mass is responsible for a lot more than decomposition. Mushrooms can spread disease, but their network is also how trees "talk" to one another.

An interesting fact about forests: root systems send water to trees most in need, even when the tree is a different species. Mycelium facilitates the transfer. I'm personifying, but I can't escape the moral message: a forest is networked through a foreign species that helps keep the diversity of that forest intact.

One of the worst things for a forest is monoculture. The same holds true for grasses. Despite taking a hit with seasonal allergies, moving from Los Angeles to Oregon provided an ecological boon. Oregon produces 650 million pounds of cool-season grass seed annually, making it the largest supplier in the world. The diversity of grasses and forests here is astounding.

Now, the irony. The American dream, given form as a post-Depression psychological motivation tool, consists of upward mobility in the style of a nice house, white picket fence, vibrant green lawn. That lawn comes at an expense: monograsses are horrible for the environment. Planting one type of seed is ecological suicide. A dominant species inevitably results in the destruction of other species as well as its own. This is as true in front yards as it is in forests as it is in oceans. Ecosystems thrive in diverse climates. They die when that diversity is crushed.

If you would have told me in college that, while writing a memoir 30 years later, I'd have to discuss the importance of diversity, I'd have laughed the thought away. My bias, sure. It just seemed so obvious at the time, living in the place of an extremely diverse college campus and in the mental space of dozens of new friends from everywhere. I was soaking in their stories while writing my own, rapidly expanding my mind through new networks. The broader culture seemed to be bending in that direction as well. Following college I spent 12 years working and living in New York City, a network of neighborhoods from every nation on the earth. My bias was strengthened even more.

Appearances deceive. There I was, living on an isolated island in the bowels of Piscataway, my mind torn open by the texts of learned people and tales of learning people, believing the future is fast approaching. Only later would I feel the full force of white grievance, the lethal reliability of an empire. Diversity, of skin tone and thought tone, isn't tolerated in many places or spaces. Not a uniquely American mindset; all cultures have biases. I was just hoping we'd be better than whatever this is we're living through right now. I hadn't expected America's dark inside voice to become so proudly and aggressively vocal. That's on me for missing it. Maybe because I grew up in a borough of (mostly) polite white enti-tlement, I thought it would stay quiet. I treated it like a pest even though it's always been an existential threat. Unsurpris-ingly, those profiled and apprehended aren't surprised by how loud it's gotten. They could never see it as a pest or a past. They've always known what it actually is, how quickly it could destroy them.

Which is what bothers me so much about this devolution. The reflexive "white people are actually oppressed" ethos reveals the spaces such people inhabit, the places they live. Poverty of being is a real problem. Identifying and trying to correct chronic structural imbalances in society is not the same as assuming individual guilt. People who take the former seriously understand the latter is a distraction. Yet that distraction is weaponized by those who enjoy the fruits of those imbalances.

In order to understand the difference between structural imbalances and personal guilt, you need to change your place, hang out in other spaces. You don't have to inhabit them; you can never actually inhabit them. But you can learn from them, empathize, understand, do better.

As much as immediate and far-reaching change is desired, most often it's slow, cautious, incremental. Which is still worlds better than America right now. You simply can't understand the fractured reality of this country by remaining in place.

25

I've lived in over a dozen cities in four states. I have fond memories and pointed criticisms of each. Every place changes you, informs the space you inhabit.

One thing I cherish most about being from Jersey is the directness. Get to the point. Time's too valuable, stop wasting all of our time yammering about irrelevant details. Don't even try to snake your way to a point. Say it and move on. Then we'll see where we stand at the end of the sentence.

This is what I grew up with and how I communicate. Casual conversation exists provided you establish boundaries. If both parties agree to shoot the shit, great. But if you want something done, the sooner you blurt it out, the sooner it's finished. Or not. Then you find someone else to fulfill that role.

I've always been on the side of directness. I'm allergic to banter. Prelude is fine provided it doesn't drag, which it often does. This is how it goes in Jersey. Moving to New York wasn't much of a culture shock. A lot of people from a lot of places, though if you want to live there, you'll catch on quick. Besides, the architecture of the city lets you know there's no time to waste. Education by osmosis.

Los Angeles is a whole other case. People don't get to the point, they talk around it, for way too long. Again, a generalization, though more often than not true. Counting letters and words and sentences as a child forced me to create a word (and world) architecture. Ivan Van Sertima wrote about the staircase of words that builds languages. My topography is a building with many rooms. Not every hallway needs to lead to a room quickly, but it better not lead nowhere. Angelenos made me feel like bashing my head against that nowhere wall.

Geography might not be destiny but it certainly influences psychology. Many college weekends were spent driving around Manhattan. Narrow streets that barely accommodate a car, much less hundreds of people spilling onto them at every angle. Driving is a game of inches. The opposite in Los Angeles: two-lane roads wider than highways back home. Meandering is a sport, drivers laser-focused on their palm devices instead of the death machines surrounding them.

Space, as in the type that allows for meandering, isn't necessarily a bad thing. It just rarely produces directness. And when directness arrives, some people are infuriated.

26

Then a new space rushed at us.

March 15, 2020. I teach two frantic classes at Equinox in Marina del Rey. I love my Sunday morning flow. Meet up with Scott around 9 for a workout. At 10:30, I teach a fitness class called Kettlebells and ViPR; at noon, Vinyasa yoga. My most popular classes of the week. I know most everyone in those studios; a number remain friends. Here, blocks from a beautiful marina that spills into the Pacific, I feel most at home as a fitness instructor. These are the classes I miss teaching most.

Weird, that day. Everyone has questions, no one with answers. A novel virus is no small thing, especially a respiratory one. There is a dark irony in the fact that a disease targeting the lungs is what ultimately broke the brains of the wellness industry, a community that spends half its time doing breathwork and pontificating about prana.

Covid contrarians now blame epidemiologists, whose job is slow and holistic, because they didn't get the info they wanted to hear right away. Reality didn't meet their expectations. Didn't help that the dude in charge would soon tell us to drink bleach and inject UV light into our veins. At the very least, we had a capable public health system, back then, something America lost the second time dude gained power. As class ends, I tell students to stack equipment in the corner so maintenance can sanitize everything. The last time those kettlebells would be used for over a year.

March 16, 2020. No classes to teach. Nowhere to go. Callan and I gaze at our new lives. I speculate we'll be locked down until at least January, a far cry from the "few weeks" talking heads are spouting. I undershoot by months. We move our dining room table into the living room. It becomes a stand for my laptop to livestream yoga classes. Plop my mat down in the dining room, set up microphones. On Tuesday I begin donation-based classes via YouTube. For a few months, they pay the rent.

Covid lockdown is a double-edge sword. I couldn't imagine doing it with anyone but Callan. Stress was everywhere, thankfully never existential, for us at least. Writing picks up. A marketing gig feeds me more work. Teaching yoga with no one in the room, just me moving through postures and barking commands, is not joyful. The entire point is communion with others. Text messages and YouTube comments are appreciated, just not replacements. But a lifeline I'm grateful for.

My year-plus of Covid lockdown: yoga and writing, hanging with wifey and cats, cooking a lot more, working out with Scott and Melanie in their garage gym, cycling up every possible canyon on my road bike. For many in the wellness community, things went very differently.

Before we get to the paranoia that consumed so many of my peers, I need to explain how I maintained my own sanity. I need to share something good.

WATCH WHAT THEY SELL

27

The broader messages of wellness have long resonated: eat whole foods, keep stress down, sleep well, exercise regularly. One of my favorite examples of the latter is done on two wheels. Cycling might be the closest thing to a "spiritual" experience I have in my life outside of listening to music.

I owned a hybrid while living in Brooklyn. While I craved speed, I needed the flexibility of suddenly hopping a curb while riding around the city. The bike proved useful flowing through city streets, yet whenever I got lapped circling Prospect Park, I realized how much more I wanted out of gearing.

Shortly after moving to Los Angeles, I purchased a Specialized road bike for $500. Clearing inventory to make room for new models, their last bike happened to be my fit. I started riding from Santa Monica to South Bay, enjoying that extra gearing while cruising down Venice Beach, Playa del Rey, Hermosa. Yet I wasn't as comfortable riding on the west coast as in New York. As with driving, cycling in a distracted city does not make for good outcomes. I feel safer two inches from a cab than 20 feet from a Tesla. Then, in a span of a month, three friends got hit. A professional violinist was tossed from her beach cruiser when an elderly woman ran a red light in Santa Monica. She couldn't perform for over a year. A fellow fitness instructor was thrown from his motorcycle on the 10, fracturing a few small bones and keeping him out of work for weeks.

The hazard of working with your body: if you aren't healthy, you don't get paid. I'm dealing with a nagging autumn head cold while writing this chapter. Though I need to take breaks from the computer, I'm able to finish my duties with relative ease. If I was still teaching group fitness, I'd sub out my classes. No income. Missing work due to a sinus cold is part of life. Missing months because some moron staring at Instagram instead of the road is something else. After that August trifecta suffered by friends, my bike started collecting dust. I wasn't willing to risk unnecessary injuries while finding my feet in a new city.

Eight years later, Covid happened. My workout partner bought a house the same week lockdowns started. The timing was chaotic though exceptional: we had a garage to build a gym in. Lockdowns started on Monday. That day, I ordered whatever I could find online: a barbell, some free weights, functional training equipment. I scoured Facebook marketplace. A guy in South Bay was constructing makeshift squat racks out of wood. Someone in the valley had kettlebells. Our weight collection was mismatched. At one point, we were using workout bands to tie dumbbells to the barbell so we could deadlift more weight. Yet we never missed a beat in our workout schedule, adapting our program as we collected equipment.

One day I mentioned my bike, now under a solar cover on the back deck of my Palms apartment. Scott used to race mountain bikes as a teenager and also owned a road bike. A little oil and an adjustment and my bike was back in shape. The roads were empty. The timing couldn't have been better.

I'll never forget bombing down six lanes of Pico or riding from the beach up Venice Blvd and never encountering a single car. For the briefest period of time, the roads returned to cyclists. And yes, we were here long before cars, though back then horses probably hated us.

Those incredible months (incredible for that reason; I'm not trying to glorify a pandemic) allowed me to fall in love with cycling again. Growing up, I knew every square inch of Milltown thanks to my BMX. The bicycle served as a symbol of freedom, mobility, and play, three cherished qualities that invoke powerful memories. Cars eventually returned, though by then I was comfortable with the rhythm of Angeleno driving. Perhaps cautious is a better word. Justin Williams, who founded the Los Angeles-based cycling team, L39ION, once said you have to be a defensive cyclist in LA. Cutting my teeth driving and later cycling around New York City, defense was bred into me. For the next few years I avoided accidents while logging thousands of miles on my bicycle.

Despite being an infamously unwalkable city, Los Angeles offers fantastic cycling. Leaving my apartment near the corner of Venice and Overland, I endured a few miles of city riding through Beverly Hills and Westfield before hustling up canyons, where so many options exist: Franklin Canyon, Benedict Canyon, Coldwater Canyon. The 16-grade up the final stretch of Stone Canyon. The turnaround at the top of Mandeville Canyon, a half-hour up, less than 10 minutes back to Sunset. Moving toward the coast, Rustic Canyon, Temescal Canyon. The epic Topanga Canyon climb, dropping me off in Woodland Hills. I sold my Specialized for close to what I paid and invested in a carbon fiber Giant. Then I found out about Dirt Mulholland, an unfinished stretch of the famous drive filled with cyclists and runners and coyote packs. I bought a gravel bike. That opened up Will Rogers, all the fire roads in Westridge. My mileage climbed. Thirty, then 50, up to 70. I hit 90 on a blazing summer day and had to bail on a century after Kuzma and I each consumed 160 ounces of water, Gatorade, and coffee. I pissed brown for two days. Two weeks later we rode 100 on the PCH. This time I had spasms for two days, though I avoided the heat on a beautiful 70ish-degree day. Kuzma, psycho that he is, cycled 125 the next day with stronger riders. Fitness is relative. I appreciate my aging body's ability to accomplish what I want without getting caught up in unrealistic expectations. And I still push myself, within reason. Just not like that.

Cycling gets me high in a way few things do. I've felt the runner's high, but running was never my sport. Three times I trained for half-marathons; all three resulted in injuries. Twice in Brooklyn, the last while training for a half-marathon trail run in LA. With the race approaching, I decided to up my mileage in Temescal Canyon. On mile 10 of a 12-mile session, my right hip labrum became aggravated, the same spot I injured years ago in Brooklyn. Sadly, I was on the descent. The final two miles were spent hobbling down the steepest grade of the day. Callan called, wondering why I wasn't home yet. I could shuffle sideways for a few feet before needing to rest, the crablike walk the only way I could gain ground. I assured her I would make it back, which I did after spending over an hour navigating two excruciating miles to the car.

I've achieved a similar high through other means. Basketball, reading. Cycling remains unique. At some point near the end of a climb, my airways open no matter how challenging the ascent. Bel Air and Beverly Glen offer some of my favorite climbs. Pounding up Stradella or adjacent Roscamare, finding my stride with the reservoir to the east, coasting down Sepulveda. The unachievable is transformed into bliss. Hitting the peak at sunrise produces an indescribable ecstasy. I felt invincible, like I could spend hours more spinning these two wheels, forcing my screaming lungs to expand and pull the fresh coastal air into my brain. The same respiratory system that used to trap me in panic was now the engine setting me free.

I would have never gotten to know Los Angeles without

my bike. Sprawl is designed for cars. I'd been confined to a few neighborhoods in nearly nine years of living there. Lots of coastal hiking, certainly, but the canyons were elusive. The bike changed everything. After every ride I'd construct a different route to tackle. Laurel Canyon was only known to me from documentaries about folk music. Now I had a relationship with those obnoxious grades. Learned the twists and turns of Griffith Park like the back of my hand. Discovered that Riverside Rancho smells eternally like horse shit. The Valley was a mystery. Now, Burbank and Glendale and Sun Valley are burned into memory. Chatsworth and Porter Ranch shimmer like deserts. Hidden Hills is designed from dreams. Agoura Hills, Westlake Village, Calabasas. So many cities to explore, and explore I did.

That's just north. Stretches of Palos Verdes smell like horses, too. Some of my favorite climbs live at the tip of Long Beach. Bile rising as I ascend the switchbacks of Palos Verdes Drive, peaking at the San Pedro overlook, staring out at prime real estate of Trump's golf course. The man deserves so much of what he'll never get and so little of what he got, this epic view included.

Angelenos pay for their views. The pricier the hood, the more dead stares I receive. Bel Air residents emerging from behind their fortress-like fences greet me with indifference at best, horror at worst. Mostly, I trail 30-year-old trucks carrying an overload of Mexicans employed to manicure their properties. The closest climb to my apartment is Baldwin Hills, a historically Black neighborhood just southeast of Culver City. Six-mile canyon climbs these are not. A quicker, more strenuous up. I arrive to smiles and hellos, an occasional "good job." Never an accusatory stare. You can feel a community when you enter one, unlike those untouchable hills that float like a battalion of islands that both compete for attention and demand privacy. Bel-Air and Beverly Hills. Most canyons aren't *that* paranoid.

The freedom I feel climbing those hills is a stunning

contrast to the rest of the day, locked inside a third-floor apartment in a crowded city, scraping together enough money for rent and food and whatever life Callan and I can muster during a pandemic. We lost roughly three-quarters of our income in one unforgettable day. In the long run, this time works out well for us. She goes to school for UX design and switches careers, finding greater happiness and fulfillment in her new role. I'm able to focus purely on writing and, out of nowhere, podcasting, a career I had never imagined for myself.

At the time, however, life was anything but stress-free. Covid-19 booted me out of wellness while also granting me a new perspective. The industry I'd been working inside of for nearly two decades took a strange but not entirely unpredictable turn. After spending years trying to help from inside, I soon discovered an even bigger role on the outside.

28

That distance exposed an explosion of paranoia. To understand why my peers suddenly sounded like right-wing conspiracy theorists, you have to go back.

The first anti-vaxxers emerged in the late 18th century. Inoculation had just been confirmed as a medical breakthrough, leading to the coining of *vaccination*, from *vacca*, cow. The animal Edward Jenner proved his theory on. Well, not his theory, exactly. The concept predates him by at least 800 years. Ancient Chinese folk medicine suggested the following remedy for dog bites: scrape a bit of the canine's brain from their skull and slather it on your wound. The idea caught on. Variolation, used throughout Asia and Africa centuries before the refinement of vaccination, was common practice.

Religion drove the original anti-vaxxers to protest. Their version of god didn't like humans tinkering with biology, which they believed was set in stone. Playing deity could only lead to bad outcomes. A religious element persists in today's movement, helping to explain the longstanding wellness crossover. The idea that the body is a sacred temple that should never be contaminated with impurities lives at the heart of their activism. Rather than recognize the long human journey from the middle to the top of the food chain, anti-vaxxers give life to an old idea: we're actually angels waiting for our wings, not an evolution of the shit and muck of raw earth that chemistry favored.

Modern anti-vaxxers take cover by blaming malicious corporate actors injecting us with toxins. Ironically, vaccine advocates are generally not champions of for-profit healthcare or fans of the pharmaceutical profit motives. Most of us want universal healthcare. Executives dictating drug prices is antithetical to pro-science folk. Anti-vaxxers have weaponized anti-corporate sentiment to their advantage, however. They cosplay as truth warriors willing to push back against the system, when many are only funneling money into the alt-med system they favor.

I first became interested in the movement during the 2014 measles outbreak in Los Angeles. How could an easily preventable disease, one eradicated in America just over a decade prior, ravage one of the nation's two largest cities, one that prides itself on setting the cultural tone and being ahead of the curve? The answer was fairly obvious. The outbreak occurred in the wealthy Brentwood and Santa Monica enclave, filled with holistic-minded parents whose privileges blinded them to the reality of anyone not living on the west side of Los Angeles. Sadly, medical misinformation has passed as truth in this area for generations.

My first published article on anti-vax ideology dates back to 2017. A number of my colleagues fell into this camp. I treated it more like a nuisance than a danger. Little did I know.

Then, in April 2020, I read an essay by British philosopher Jules Evans about a phenomenon called conspirituality. The term was new to me; the concept wasn't. The abstract from the 2011 research paper that defined the term is worth reading in full:

> The female-dominated New Age (with its positive focus on self) and the male-dominated realm of conspiracy theory (with its negative focus on global politics) may seem antithetical. There is a synthesis of the two, however, that we call 'conspirituality'. We define, describe, and analyse this hybrid system of belief; it has been noticed before without receiving much scholarly attention. Conspirituality is a rapidly growing web movement expressing an ideology fuelled by political disillusionment and the popularity of alternative worldviews. It has international celebrities, bestsellers, radio and TV stations. It offers a broad politico-spiritual philosophy based on two core convictions, the first traditional to conspiracy theory, the second rooted in the New Age: 1) a secret group covertly controls, or is trying to control, the political and social order, and 2) humanity is undergoing a 'paradigm shift' in consciousness. Proponents believe that the best strategy for dealing with the threat of a totalitarian 'new world order' is to act in accordance with an awakened 'new paradigm' worldview.

I was acutely aware of this strange crossover between left-leaning crunchy hippies and right-wing conspiracy theorists. Today's wellness slogans are just recycled from nineties brick-and-mortar yoga spaces: *You're your own best doctor. No one knows your body better than you. The only pharmacy you need is already inside you.* Accompanying these pithy statements is a sense that Big Medicine only exists to keep us sick so that we remain lifelong customers. They must be in cahoots with Big Global Government in order to achieve their goal of world-wide subservience. To be fair, these sentiments predate that era. Americans have been uniquely anti-expert and anti-medicine since Europeans first stumbled onto these shores, lugging contrarian stances with the rest of their baggage. Boy, does our culture love a good conspiracy theory. Many bad ones, too.

A week later, I wrote an essay about conspirituality for my Big Think column. The piece hit a nerve. Mere weeks into lockdowns, every piece of content, for better and worse, had a chance of going viral. Everyone was glued to their devices, seeking answers, searching for content, looking for any distraction possible. Since many turned to social media to learn about news, an entire cohort of wellness influencers metamorphosed into political commentators, taking their massive following along for the ride. Some slid into an conspiratorial indoctrination path along with their favorite influencers while a whole bunch us thought *what the fuck*. We found answers in this wellness-to-right pipeline.

Here's how I framed it in that article:

A lack of critical thinking has long plagued the wellness community. An example: Since herbs and tinctures can be sold as dietary supplements with minimal federal oversight, companies go to great lengths to advertise their products regardless of clinical evidence. This has resulted in a multi-billion dollar alternative medicine market. If you want to achieve success in this market, you need to be alternative to something. That something happens to be vaccines, and Big Pharma in general.

Not that Big Pharma isn't an appropriate enemy. The for-profit medical model is not designed to serve our interests. A real conspiracy is the relationship between pharmaceutical companies and doctors fostered by lackluster federal oversight. We should be up in arms about a mental health crisis that has in large part been created for profit maximization. But that story is complex and our brains are not designed to process complexity. An easier target is vaccines, one of the most effective and important scientific advances in history.

You may have picked up on the fact that I was simmering

in my own conspiracy: collusion between doctors and pharma to monetize mental health distress. While I still believe antidepressants are sometimes overprescribed, and I'd prefer a system where everyone has access to talk therapy, conversations with people that have been greatly helped by pharmaceutical interventions helped me understand the error of my thinking. As clinical psychologist Jonathan Stea told me, antidepressants are just one tool in his profession's toolkit. Some doctors will abuse it. Good ones do not.

Conspirituality was a relatively untapped field of study when I stumbled into the term. An opportunity to pursue it further arose two weeks later when the anti-vax pseudodocumentary, *Plandemic*, was released online. My article might have garnered a million views, but this propaganda film took off into the stratosphere, with the director later unironically calling it the "most censored documentary ever" while claiming it was seen by more people than any other documentary in history.

Don't worry if these claims don't match up. Little in contrarian wellness spaces does.

The notion that "natural" is better than "pharmaceutical" has long been a galvanizing cry in the anti-vax movement. *Plandemic* filmmaker Mikki Willis buys into that sentiment. During the 2014 outbreak Willis lived in the hippie enclave of Ojai. While I'm not aware of his vaccination beliefs at that time, by 2020 he was fully radicalized.

His short film couldn't have arrived at a better time for that movement. A perpetually online public was seeking any clarity possible. Anti-vax activists were ready to muddy the waters with their contrarian truth: the pandemic was *really* a psy-op created by the one-world government to control the population and force pharmaceuticals down our throats. Never mind that we were nearly a year away from a Covid vaccine hitting the market. They just knew it was going to be deadly. In the long run mRNA fit the bill, even if any intervention would have been shoehorned into their agenda. Even though mRNA was first developed in the late eighties and the first mRNA-based vaccine was tested in humans in 2011, they latched onto "experimental jab" to spread fear and uncertainty around Covid vaccines.

I had a hunch Willis's propaganda flick was going to take off, and boy, did it. On May 6, I published an article pointing out seven glaring flaws in the film, which would also get over a million page views. A drop in the bucket. People were already distrustful of the government. Our president was telling us to drink bleach and inject light into our bodies. Conspiracy theories, always simmering under the surface of American society, explode during times of crisis. The anti-vax army had been building in force and volume since Andrew Wakefield fabricated a 1998 study about a supposed link between vaccines and autism. This was their moment, and did they ever capitalize.

At the time, I produced an occasional podcast called *Earth-Rise*. Mostly interviews for my Big Think column and interesting conversations with friends. I reached out to fellow Angeleno and yoga instructor Julian Walker, who I had launched a project with in 2012 called *YogaBrains*. Founded by five local teachers, the blog was meant to inspire political engagement in the yoga community. We ran it for over a year until it petered out. Wellness practitioners weren't willing to accept their practices had a political dimension. Matthew Remski was a contributor to that site. I contacted him about coming onto my podcast to discuss *Plandemic* as well. We recorded that Thursday; I immediately posted it. Something interesting happened.

EarthRise averaged a couple hundred downloads per episode. This one quickly jumped into the thousands, accompanied by hundreds of comments on Facebook. I asked them to return the following week. That one also went well; downloads and comments surged. I mentioned the success of my article on conspirituality, how no one has explored the concept in any depth. We agreed to make it a weekly project, one that has grown immensely since.

The fact that we have different backgrounds in wellness proved to be a strength. All three of us taught yoga. We all "drank the juice" to varying degrees. While we still find value in wellness practices today, we're critical of certain dynamics within these spaces. Matthew often focuses on cults and leftist politics; Julian, on political movements and philosophy. For me, the main dynamic I explore is healthism (an excessive focus on personal health as a primary moral good) present in wellness culture. Many influencers share a belief that health is primarily (if not completely) in your control. I also cover health and science misinformation extensively.

While healthism has long persisted in America, Ronald Reagan pushed it to the forefront of national consciousness. His economic philosophy, Reaganomics, is based on deregulation. Push as many social services into the private market as possible. Decimate New Deal reforms. To help accomplish this, Reaganomics teaches that health largely or completely depends on individual choices. That way, you can't blame social forces for bad outcomes. A convenient way to sidestep universal healthcare: why should everyone pay for your personal failures? Where Reagan left off, the Heritage Foundation picked up. Project 2025 pushes for healthcare privatization more than the Gipper ever did.

Experts disagree that health is purely individual. The social determinants of health encompass non-individual factors affecting personal health. Education level, income, healthcare access, race, gender, and environmental factors play essential roles. Some experts believe more than half of individual health depends on these factors. Yet wellness influencers overwhelmingly ignore or downplay them. They favor the bootstraps philosophy of health: lifestyle factors like diet, sleep, exercise, supplements, and faith are all that matter. Indeed, while some of them absolutely matter (pushing supplements and faith off to the side) they don't tell the entire story.

According to these influencers, social inequities aren't relevant in our supposedly egalitarian society. We all have the same opportunities on a level playing field, right? We're all free in this democracy, ain't we? Plus, they've struggled as well. Personal adversities are often placed front and center in the narratives they construct when building wellness brands. They overcame the gauntlet they had to run through. Why can't everyone else?

I'm not discounting anyone's struggles. An anecdote provides a limited amount of data, however. The more consumed a person is with their own story, the less likely they'll consider the struggles of others. And if they're beneficiaries of a system they believe is oppressing them, they're not going to wrap their minds around the real-world suffering of others. Those Angeleno parents in 2014 truly believed everyone could purchase fresh produce at Whole Foods after yoga and heal their problems with cleansing and intentions. I know because they took my classes.

Back here in reality, we're all beneficiaries of public health, a system that works best when undetected. Preventive medicine results in illnesses you never suffer from. Modern wellness is filled with protocols and products designed to stave off disease, many geared toward "boosting" your immune system. Yet one of the cheapest and most effective preventive interventions, vaccines, is the main target of their suspicion and derision. Vaccines train the immune system to fend off disease later on, the same feat the supplements, protocols, and "detoxes" influencers market supposedly accomplish. Despite claims that their products are natural (and therefore "good" or "right," the moral dimension of healthism), many are produced through the same chemical processes as the pharmaceuticals they decry. Yet they love *some* pharmaceuticals, like ivermectin and hydroxychloroquine. Testosterone replacement therapy for the dudes. Peptides all over. A touch of Botox and fillers to keep the natural glow. All manufactured by Big Pharma. Everything is chemistry, an inconvenient truth they prefer to ignore.

Many amazing people operate in the wellness industry. My critiques revolve around two major problems. First, misinformation. Spreading nonsense about clinical studies, and also claiming wellness products are evidence-based. While I have a billion problems with for-profit healthcare, clinical testing is not one of them. If supplement manufacturers had to endure the same proof of efficacy as pharmaceutical companies, we wouldn't be discussing the trillion-dollar wellness industry.

The second involves the extreme messages by influencers and contrarians, which they market in order to make their positions seem reasonable. Seed oils are not toxic. Sunscreen is not toxic. Statins are not toxic. Celery juice is not a cure-all. Berberine is not nature's Ozempic. Coffee enemas are not healthier than drinking coffee. John D Rockefeller did not fund the pharmaceutical industry in order to find more uses for petroleum.

If any or all of those sentences are confusing, congratulations. You're not swimming in the waters I push against on a daily basis. Tragically, they are, alongside hundreds more like them, part of a surging wellness mindset being exploited, weaponized, and monetized by an upper tier of wellness influencers and political contrarians that coalesced in MAHA. And all of our health is at risk because of them.

29

But MAHA tells one hell of a story.

On its face, Kennedy's movement is about making people healthier. Calls for reforming the American healthcare system rise loudly from their pulpit. Entwined with numerous other domains (environmental factors, income, education, infrastructure, workplace regulations) a systemic overhaul is required to make a dent in the nation's health outcomes. MAHA leaders claim to desire such an overhaul, then consistently do the opposite.

Yet they spin a compelling story, and humans are storytelling animals. Where actual change happens, through legislation and regulations, is fodder for bureaucracies that rarely gain public attention. My first reporting job required attending zoning board, town council, and school board meetings in Monroe, a suburb just south of my hometown. These meetings are where the wheels of bureaucracy are greased. Issues that affect the entire town are made here. In a town of roughly 50,000 people, maybe 10 residents showed up to any of them. Even then, some only showed up to complain about sanitation workers misplacing their garbage cans or too many Black people roaming their neighborhood (both true stories). Time and again, I watched citizens grow angry when a new building began construction. When asked whether or not they attended the zoning board meeting in which this project was discussed, the result was a blank stare.

MAHA has created a livelier (though fabricated) story about health, removing all the pesky bureaucracy stuff. Administrative jobs are presented as wasteful bloat. Few tears were shed when Kennedy oversaw the firing of tens of thousands of public health workers, actively defunded research into the social determinants of health, and dismantled the very departments tackling the problems he claims to care about. Taking a cue from Reaganomics, MAHA's focus is individual health: airport gyms, performance-enhancing supplements, the "suppression of sunshine." Totally irrelevant when it comes to the nuts and bolts of public health, though sexy as fuck to a wellness culture attuned to slathering tallow as sunscreen and sunning their assholes. (Look it up.) (Wait, don't.) Provided the conversation points to a deep state in collusion with evil corporations, Kennedy's acolytes believe they're rebelling against the empire, even as they tweet from the Death Star.

Stories reveal unseen forces simmering under reality. Let's pull back from MAHA for a moment to zone back in. The 19th century brought a wave of academics interested in connecting cultures. Evolving communications and media technologies enabled more scholarship, and oftentimes more speculation about foreign lands and ideas. James George Frazer and Joseph Estlin Carpenter helped spearhead the field of comparative religious studies that would influence Joseph Campbell and Mircea Eliade. These men were trying to identify threads that weave together the fabric of humanity's stories. Noble in nature, their works weren't without problems, as later criticisms of Campbell's monomyth show. That's the nature of knowledge, however: it builds on itself. Campbell flattened some cultures he encountered, though he wasn't working with 21st-century tools. That doesn't make his work less valuable for the time it was created in.

The drive toward telling the "story of everything" also evolved, though usually not in flattering ways. Books like Ken Wilber's *A Theory of Everything: An Integral Vision for Business, Politics, Science and Spirituality* attempted to shoehorn, well, everything into a neatly packaged thesis that just happens to fit into his own personal metatheory. He's not alone. Sri Aurobindo blended spirituality with evolutionary theory and social philosophy when creating Integral Yoga; Stanislav Grof created transpersonal psychology as a vehicle for integrating consciousness research with spirituality and psychotherapy; and neuroscientist Francisco Varela concocted his enactive theory to bridge biology, phenomenology, and consciousness studies.

This abbreviated list includes a few thinkers whose work made a cultural impact. Downstream people haphazardly develop their own throw-it-all-together philosophies, which they freely share in spaces like yoga classes. Wilber and Aurobindo were particularly influential in these spaces due to their emphasis on spirituality. Little is more salable than claiming a unified field of knowledge exists just beyond the grasp of the meat suits we trudge through life wearing. Sprinkle in mysticism and your chances for a hit increase.

Take Paramahansa Yogananda. Whether or not his teacher purposefully perished in order to animate a dead body, as he claims in *Autobiography of a Yogi*, is irrelevant. The body continues the conversation with the young yogi, instructing him like Krishna did Arjuna. This channeled lesson made Yogananda one of the most famous (and richest) yogis in the nation. Hell of a story regardless of facts, echoing classical mythologies from India.

Here's where things inevitably go off the rails. By this point, a decision must be made: understand the story metaphorically or treat it as a historical fact. Transcending the mundane is a seductive prospect. As with most mythologies, a moral or philosophical lesson is often addressed. The metaphor, in the form of a story, provides an imaginative way to deliver a lesson. One of the great values of mythology.

Or you take it literally. People do. The most common defense: *How do you know it didn't happen?* A thought-terminating cliché disguised as inquiry. Anecdotes are impossible to disprove. We're left to piece together the puzzle through scientific inquiry, in this case anthropology and biology. Devotees shit on materialistic disciplines like that, preferring to engage with a dimension that "can't be measured" but they're certain exists.

We're currently at the most advanced stage of science in history. In another generation, provided no catastrophic event occurs, we'll be even further along. To believe a dead body can be reanimated requires not only an incredible leap of faith, but an outright denial of thousands of years of acquired knowledge. The notion that this could have occurred in a near-distant or ancient time requires a dramatic rewriting of biology, one which we have no documentation of.

I get that's why they call it "faith," but come on. What would such a feat even signify? What social function would it serve? A parallel example: channelers, people who claim to talk to deceased individuals, aliens, or spirits. I've listened to hundreds of hours of their "transmissions" for *Conspirituality*. Every time, without fail, they "return" with completely irrelevant messages. They never offer anything useful, such as cures for diseases or plans to solve pressing geopolitical issues. Never about creating equity in society. Almost always something their followers want to hear. I would think an ancient alien god with limitless knowledge would throw us a bone once in a while, but nada.

Imagining an invisible mini-me fleeing this meat suit might sound compelling. There's not much harm in such flights of imagination. Until you threaten to kill anyone who doesn't believe in your invisible mini-me. Stories become powerful motivators for people to fuck up other people. The religious side of things.

There's a bigger problem. Religious thinking tends to spill over into other domains. Like health. The same suspension of disbelief that occurs in spirituality impacts our understanding of bodies. Ideas about a pure spirit nestled inside muscle and organs has led to an incredible amount of medical misinformation. When misinformation about successful public health interventions results in policy changes that promote the spread of viruses (a la Kennedy), a whole lot of damage can be done. The problem is twofold: the products influencers sell are often ineffective (and at times dangerous) and the interventions they keep you from taking can lead to serious health consequences.

Early in *Conspirituality*, I devised a heuristic for understanding how the wellness grift works: watch what they say, then watch what they sell. If an influencer speaks negatively about statins, then hits you with an affiliate link for a natural solution to cholesterol, their true intention becomes clear. You just have to listen for the signal within the noise of their story.

Years after *Plandemic* dropped, Mikki Willis launched his own line of "immune support" supplements. Unlike vaccines, which undergo years of rigorous testing on hundreds of thousands of people, Willis's product has never been tested. In August 2025, he held a webinar to pitch his supplement line. The premise was to "share stories," though every tale somehow circled back to his product. Willis likes to indulge his heroism on 9/11, even though it's tough to pin down how long he was at ground zero, what he did, or how he helped. Regardless, the anecdote makes its way into many appearances, including this webinar:

> A healthy mind makes good decisions, and a good decision then helps you through these tragedies in such a way that doesn't necessarily have to become PTSD or something that takes you years to heal from. And I know this simply because when I was at the World Trade Center, a lot of people I was with didn't fare as well as I did. But it was a conscious choice I made while on the rubble to make sure that I looked at this environment with gratitude, as horrible as it was, to find a purpose and what I call divine consciousness in this situation. And that mindset, that perspective, is what got me through that without dealing with what a lot of people that I was with that are either dead now or very sick are dealing with. And so we've created this, because as most of you, we actually for that purpose, we created an immune formula that we're, we have an offer we'll extend later.

Think about what's happening here. Willis is comparing his own who-knows-how-long experience in lower Manhattan with people who spent months digging through rubble for dead bodies following one of the worst tragedies in modern American history. Besides making such an asinine, heartless statement—to then immediately pitch an untested supplement, no less—his claim is that he avoided getting sick because he was grateful. The implication is that people who got sick or died failed to have gratitude. *They failed to have the right mindset.*

Willis's sentiment represents the highest level of

douchebaggery. But the general idea, *right thinking equals right health*, is sadly pervasive in wellness. It makes perfect sense that Willis's propaganda film was secretly funded by Kennedy, and that Willis championed Kennedy's ascension to Secretary of HHS. Both men share the same goal: dismantling America's public health system by replacing it with the power of their stories.

30

They've weaponized their story. The only way to fight back is to tell a better one, or at least force theirs into the light. That's how I ended up in Palm Beach in November 2025, just a few miles from Mar-a-Lago.

Eudemonia Summit was launched in 2024 in an attempt to merge wellness and science. Laudable mission, though the money is certainly in wellness, which the organizers lean into. Keynote speakers included Andrew Huberman and Mark Hyman, two wellness market giants who regularly blur the line between science and marketing. Sometimes they get science right, often wrong, quite wrong. Something is usually sold by the end of the podcast, or at the beginning. Sometimes the entire podcast is a sales pitch. If you're not accustomed to critically reviewing transcripts, it's damn near impossible to know where science begins and where speculation enters. Obscuring that line sadly seems to be part of their technique.

I applaud the inclusion of people critical of wellness practices in the programming, which led to my invitation. Besides a solo talk on misinformation, I recorded a live podcast with Dr Jessica Knurick, a registered dietitian who's become one of the most successful science communicators of our time. With an academic background focused on chronic disease, she makes a perfect foil against MAHA's rhetoric. Unlike those influences, she holds a doctorate that began with a focus on combating chronic disease. She regularly discusses the social determinants of health, advocating for actual systemic change that benefits those who need access to nutritious foods and healthcare most.

I was also invited to take part in two debates. On Saturday, I sat on stage with self-proclaimed "godfather of biohacking," Dave Asprey, to discuss seed oils. The following day, I debated fluoride with biological dentist Dominik Nischwitz. These conversations encapsulate many of the feelings, gimmicks, and trends in wellness I've reviewed on *Conspirituality* for years.

Let's start on the conference floor.

Throughout the early- to mid-aughts, I traveled to wellness conferences to DJ parties sponsored by a collection of "superfood" companies: Sambazon, Guayaki, Manitoba Harvest, Dr Bronner's, and other brands defining their products around specific ingredients, like acai, yerba mate, and hemp. Like a lot of wellness brands at that time, they marketed their products as part of a healthy lifestyle. The imagery was empowering, the colors fun. While they sometimes used science-sounding language, they generally led with messages designed to trigger positive emotions. And, like all marketing, the opening of wallets.

Over the ensuing decades, I watched wellness marketing shift from empowerment to fear. While this trend picked up dramatically during the pandemic, it was set in motion years before. A weird juxtaposition emerged: many wellness devotees claim that health is not political, yet their marketing materials track national politics. In one generation, wellness went from practices designed for your highest self to products sold through fear.

A few on display at Eudemonia: Fear toxins. Buy this spray. Fear lead. Buy this protein. Fear fat. Buy this "natural GLP-1." Fear fluoride. Buy this toothpaste. Fear being unoptimal. Buy this peptide. Fear seed oils. Buy this butter. Buy these tallow chips. Buy this protein water. (Yes, there's protein water.)

Those items fit into your bag. The large-ticket items were

even more baffling. Not gonna lie, the robot masseuse was something. But the red light tanning bed that pumps hydrogen into the chamber during your Matrix-style longevity session? The company set up an Airstream housing just one bed. The target audience must be clinics, though I'm sure a few attendees have the space and budget for a $60,000 gadget that's totally science-backed.

I'm not against any of this, per se. I ate the tallow chips. I wasn't going to get into the chamber, though I would have hopped into the mobile sauna if it wasn't so crowded. Nothing wrong with getting your sweat on and eating nutritious food. The promise of science when you're selling speculation irks me. Market your sauna for feeling good all you want. Just quit telling me this peptide is going to extend my life when we both know you're talking out of your ass.

Speaking of, Dave Asprey. Dude made a killing from throwing butter into coffee. His origin story has him nourished by yak butter tea while scaling the Himalayas. Maybe, though critics point out that buttered coffee was already in circulation in the Crossfit community. Not surprised Asprey would co-opt a hunch. His degree is in computer information systems, not biology, not nutrition. He doesn't do research, he (maybe) reads it then jumps to conclusions.

I open the debate by talking about food access. The gap between MAHA's messaging and the reality of their legislation. Kennedy led the charge in getting soda and candy removed from some state SNAP benefits, which over 42 million Americans rely on. Ultra-processed foods are contributing to our chronic disease epidemic, the thinking goes. Not wrong. Foodstuffs aren't great for health, though in moderation there's little wrong with them. Kennedy will never admit that. He stands on stage waxing poetic about farmer's markets and wholesome food. But he never closes the gap. Food is removed from SNAP; nothing replaces it. MAHA leaders claim the food is coming, trust me, like all politicians who will accomplish amazing things if only you vote for them. Then disappear when your vote is cast.

Asprey says seed oils aren't food, they're poison, never to be consumed. He waxes poetic about how "the people" need to be fed properly. I laugh, telling him it's the first time I've ever heard him address the proletariat. (True to form, he still shits on oatmeal during our debate, which he's repeatedly called "peasant food." Coming from a lineage of Eastern European peasants, he can fuck right off.) We both agree ultraprocessed foods aren't great. We both agree food deserts suck, that whole foods should be both accessible and affordable. Then I ask about the gap. Wishing away poverty isn't how it will be fixed. Demanding healthy food be made available to everyone requires policy. He punts. Talks about a pricey olive oil company he thinks is "doing it right." I mention how selective eating leads to eating disorders. He pivots to First Amendment rights. Then Second Amendment rights. I tell him using his platform to spread misinformation as a sales funnel is wildly irresponsible. I don't mention that the First Amendment is a protection against state persecution, not a bulwark against woke. I chuckle when he mentions the Second Amendment, mostly because it's so damn expectable when you don't have an actual argument.

Social services don't help an influencer's bottom line. Better for them to claim their products are the key to real health and avoid all that policy stuff. In fact, during my debate with Nischwitz, I mentioned health is political. He shakes his head no, he doesn't believe that. Health is what you put into your body, what you do with your body. Influencers never seem to factor in the fact that what you put into and do with your body has a lot to do with societal forces.

I'll extend Dominik a little grace. He lives in Germany, a country with much stronger social safety nets than America. That said, his country has made health quite political in the not-too-distant past. Also, no society is utopia. Health and politics are inescapable aspects of civilization. The best we can hope for is closing the gap as much as possible. Listening to grown men wrongly demonize seed oils and fluoride while selling alternative products is the biggest problem with modern wellness.

Not even the selling bothers me. It's how they sell, and what's lost in the process: the simple, unsexy reality of having a human body that ages, aches, and eventually breaks down. A reality you can't biohack your way out of.

WELL ENOUGH

31

My 50th birthday brought me the gift of plantar fasciitis.

For years, students would tell me about their challenges with this stabbing pain, the lengths they had to go to mitigate the tenderness. The massaging, the stretching, the cortisone shots. You can empathize but not understand. Until it finds you, that is.

That's my right foot. Around the same time, I began having a sharp pain in my left big toe. X-rays discovered a bone spur. My podiatrist showed me how to manage plantar fasciitis, which I've continued to do, to varying success. If I don't keep up with the exercises, that sharp pain rushes back. The spur is only manageable until I need surgery, if I want to go that route. I'm not ready to give in yet. I feel lucky that it's available to me, if necessary.

The frustration is the worst part. I began wearing minimalist footwear over 20 years ago. Nothing started a subway conversation like toe shoes. People asked all sorts of questions, made all sorts of assumptions. I always respond the same way: you think cramming your toes together in modern footwear is good for your feet? I never understood the chronic obsession with small feet, but men have fucked up biomechanics for centuries. And yes, it's always been beauty standards created by men.

Closer to home, running shoes defined the tight toe box. Gen Xers grew up thinking that restricting half your foot is simply how they were meant to be managed. Created tons of work for podiatrists, as well as doctors and joint specialists all the way up the chain of the body. What happens to your feet affects everything else.

Confronting two foot problems at once (three, counting the plantar wart that initially prompted the visit) shook me. As a writer, I sit a lot, mitigated by a standing desk. But I'm also quite active and intend on remaining so. Plantar fasciitis often occurs due to changing movement patterns. Getting a puppy resulted in a lot more walking. Recurring pain during each evening stroll was not in my plans, but a lot of health outcomes aren't planned. You do the best you can with what you have, then attend to things as they pop up.

Like anxiety. While eating meat stopped panic attacks, I've been struggling with sleep lately. Not sleeping itself, just falling asleep. Might be apnea. While drifting, I'll feel a jolt of electricity and jump awake, sometimes gasping for breath. Using a strip of heavy-duty tape to open my nose has helped immensely, though one evening it was bad bad. I slept maybe three hours. At times, I feared I was having a stroke. Turns out that breathing difficulties while at rest can produce psychedelic mental states, which is basically what I was experiencing. Without any of the benefits of psychedelics, sadly.

Once again, it all comes back to respiration. Decades after my first panic attacks, after all the yoga, the canyon climbs, the respiratory pandemic, my body is just reminding me of the one biological truth I can't hack: you have to fight for every breath.

I went to my doctor the next day. I told her my history

with anxiety, the exact feelings I've been having. She asked questions. I floated the possibility of nocturnal hypertension, something I read about while furiously typing my symptoms into a chatbot. I promised I'm not Dr Google, or Dr AI, but the symptoms lined up. She said it was certainly a possibility, though she thought it pertinent to draw blood first. We developed a plan together. The bloodwork showed nothing abnormal, so she ordered a sleep study next, then a 24-hour blood pressure test to rule out nocturnal hypertension.

Basically, everything Kennedy and his MAHA coalition say isn't happening in modern medicine: empathy, care, informed consent. Sometimes when I listen to wellness influencers speak, I wonder what planet they live on. I've had shitty doctors, too. And I've experienced way too many headaches dealing with insurance companies and hospital systems. But I've also been the recipient of exceptional, thoughtful care, something I would never expect from an online influencer with no training.

Aging is the most humbling endeavor we'll ever embark on. And democratizing: no one avoids it.

Wellness and fitness are powerful antidotes. They're temporary, though extremely important. True, my exercise sessions are driven as much by neurosis as genuine love of movement, sometimes one taking the lead, sometimes the other. I've come to terms with the fact that I'll always have to balance the two. Decline is inevitable but it doesn't have to be rapid. Bright spots trail dedication. When getting my first colonoscopy at 48, the nurses couldn't believe I wasn't on a single medication. They actually called others over to talk about it.

I don't know how to feel about avoiding medications at this age, or the fact that so many others haven't. It's not a judgment. We all grapple with health in our own ways. I'm lucky in certain ways, not so much in others. But it did remind me to keep moving, keep cooking, keep stress down, and sleep a full night. To remember that life is a blessing and this is the one shot we've got, so make the most of it. To take care of myself to the best of my ability, for as long as I have a body. To let go of optimizing and hacking and unrealistic expectations. To remind myself, every day, that well enough is enough.

ACKNOWLEDGMENTS

The impact of the wellness industry has been profound. Thank you to all teachers, students, and listeners for guidance, love, feedback, and criticism. May we all grow stronger together.

To Matthew Remski and Julian Walker for six years of *Conspirituality*, a career pivot I could have never predicted and value every day. To our fearless colleague, Mallory DeMille, for the daily content chats. And to the hundreds of guests, experts, and friends I've made fighting misinformation since a pandemic broke so many brains.

To my family and a lifetime of close friends, written about with love in these pages. Not all of you were mentioned, though there will be more memoirs.

To Callan for 12 incredible years and counting, and the family we've built: Baltasar, Magellan, and Tempo (RIP Osiris and Anula). May we always be surrounded by amazing animals for as long as we're here.

ABOUT THE AUTHOR

Derek Beres is a multi-faceted author, speaker, and podcaster based in Portland, Oregon. His reporting has appeared in *The NY Times*, *The Guardian*, *Mother Jones*, *Rolling Stone*, *Playboy*, and *Time*.

He has served in senior editorial positions at a number of tech companies and has decades of experience in health, science, and music writing.

Derek regularly speaks on science and media literacy. He is the co-host of the Conspirituality podcast.

derekberes.com